# Quilting

## THE WORLD OVER

# Quilting
## THE WORLD OVER

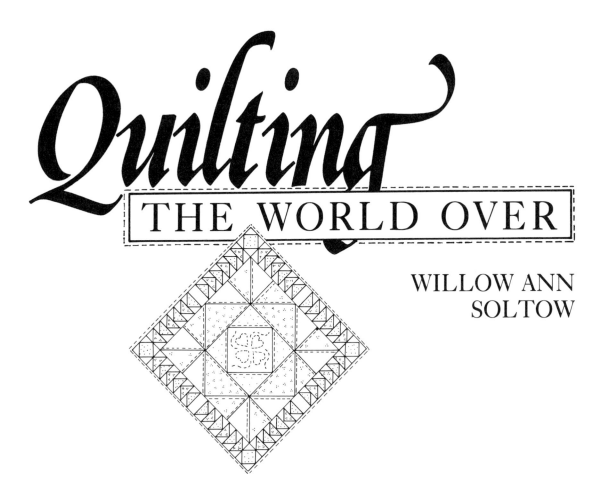

WILLOW ANN
SOLTOW

Chilton Book Company
Radnor, Pennsylvania

Published in Radnor, Pennsylvania 19089, by Chilton Book Company

Designed by Anthony Jacobson
Color and black and white photographs by Jim Conroy,
except where otherwise credited.
Line illustrations by Willow Soltow and Anthony Jacobson.
Manufactured in the United States of America

Library of Congress Cataloging in Publication Data

Soltow, Willow Ann.
    Quilting the world over / by Willow Ann Soltow.
        p.    cm.
    Includes bibliographical references and index.
    ISBN 0-8019-8028-3 (pb.)
    1. Machine quilting—Patterns.   2. Patchwork—Patterns.
    I. Title.
    TT835.S626    1990                        90-55320
    746.46—dc20                               CIP

1 2 3 4 5 6 7 8 9 0    9 8 7 6 5 4 3 2 1

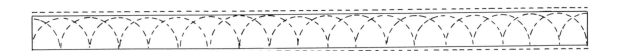

# To
Dr. Emily Jayne,
who never made a quilt in her life
and quite possibly never will.

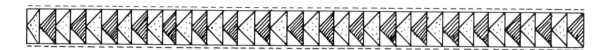

# Contents

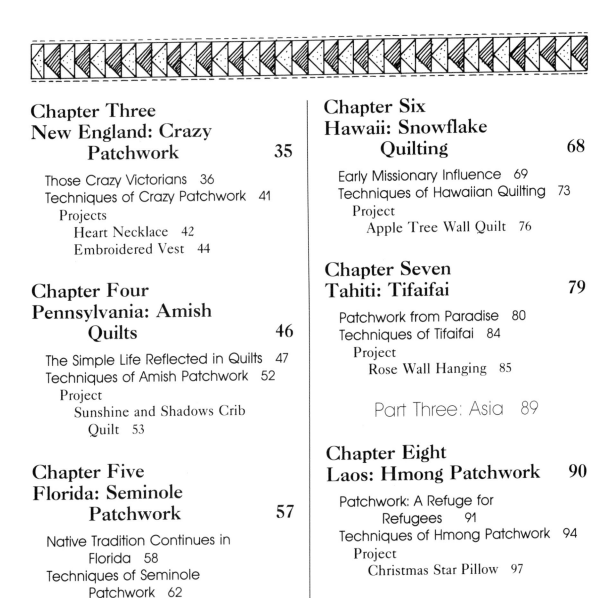

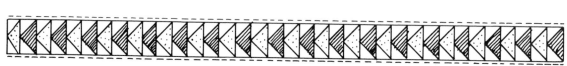

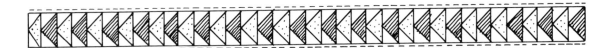

# Recommended Reading   188

# Supplies and Suppliers   192

# Templates for Projects   196

# Index   223

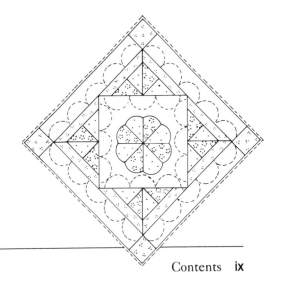

# Acknowledgments

The information and illustrations in a book of this scope could not have been brought together without the cooperation and active enthusiasm of a great many people. It is my pleasure to gratefully acknowledge my parents Bill and Shirley Soltow for their loving and constant support as well as my grandmother Helen Winona Martin for her warm encouragement. I wish to thank the sisters of my sewing circle for their willing hands—Martha Viehmann, Bina Williams, Susan Malter, and in particular Robin Buckingham for sewing assistance, modeling, and photo research. Special thanks to her husband Douglas Fleming for his photography. I am also very grateful to John Dojka for his assistance in producing the final manuscript.

I owe a special debt to the following people who have given so generously of their time: Barbara Jane Hale for introducing me to the needleworkers at the Seminole Indian Reservation in Immokolee, Florida; Rob Spencer for his photography and for being an extra pair of hands at sewing; Marjorie Agosin for her comments and expertise on Chilean arpilleras; Nancy Thompson for her observations on West African culture; and Yvonne Wardwell of the Stamford Historical Society for her tireless assistance.

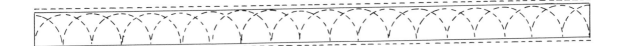

I am very grateful to Paul McGuire of Yale University for giving me the idea of using Penrose tiles in quiltmaking and for his efforts to help me get in touch with their originator. I am also much obliged to Dr. Roger Penrose of the University of Oxford for graciously permitting the use of his patented tiles. Warm thanks also to Robert Field for his expert insights on and photographs of Romano-British floor mosaics.

I am especially grateful to the following people who kindly allowed me to photograph examples from their collections or permitted the use of their photographs: Barbara White, David M. Schwartz, David Sacco, Linda Behar, Judy Matheison, Louise Young, Lynn Lloyd of the American Quilter's Society, Jane Wilk Sterry of Patches and Patchwork, Bonnie Benjamin of Needleworks International, and Kenneth Pellman and the people at Good Books.

My thanks to Elizabeth Akana for her suggestions and to Mrs. Lee S. Wild of the Mission Houses Museum for her help. Heartfelt thanks to Daniel R. Brauer of Fowler Museum of Cultural History, UCLA for his kind assistance.

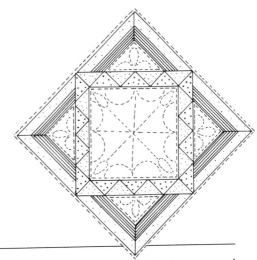

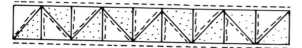

# Introduction

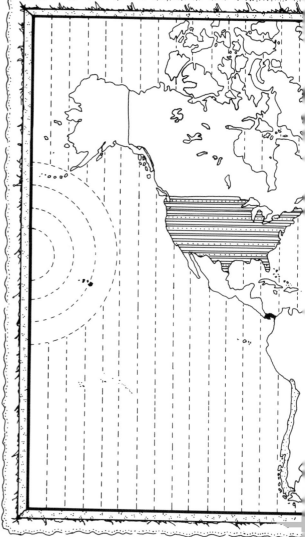

We are poised on the threshold of a global age. Today, we are just beginning to think of ourselves as planetary citizens. It is a new way of thinking and one in which we will have to become adept before long—our world depends on it. Today, the destruction of thirty acres of rain forest in Brazil brings the loss of songbirds in North America; the strengthening of the yen in Tokyo means that a dollar buys less in New York City. The interconnections are endless.

Global thinking promises to be a real challenge for some of us who already have enough difficulty with local thinking—putting out the garbage on time and remembering the week's PTA meeting. Our descendents will no doubt look back on our age as being hopelessly primitive. But to us it is a miraculous time which has seen the dismantling of the Berlin Wall, the hope of eliminating nuclear weapons, and the development of understanding through improved communications.

In such an age, quiltmaking has its place. Every stitch taken in a creative spirit is an answer to despair; every knotted thread an affirmation of peaceful human endeavor. Historically, throughout the world, women's needlework has been regarded as a documentation of life's activities. It has allowed women to preserve and to communicate their deepest emotions and convictions. In some countries, Chile for instance, needlework has actually played a viable role in the human struggle for freedom and unity.

This book is not intended to be an exhaustive study of the places, peoples and needlework techniques presented. Such a

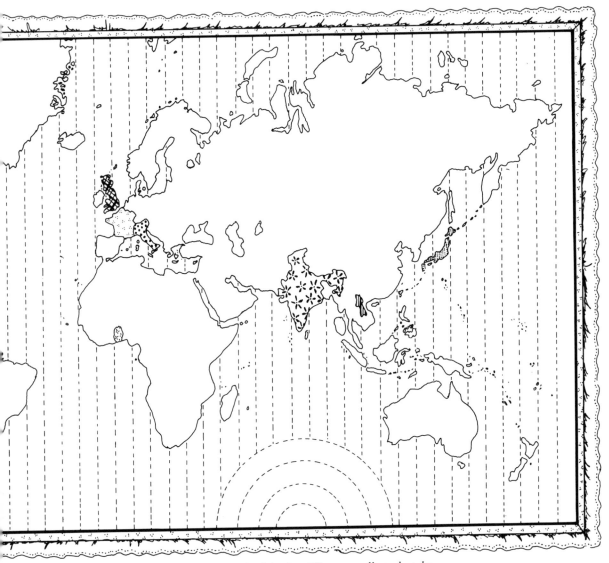

*Fig. I-1. World map showing areas of origin for different needlework styles.*

work would extend far beyond the scope of a single volume. Instead, it is offered as a modest exercise in global thinking. It is meant as a bridge between our culture and other cultures; between our times and those to come—in which we must dedicate ourselves to our planet and the people and animals who share it. After all, the needle was invented to bind things together.

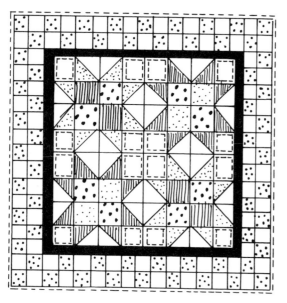

# Chapter One

# Basic Techniques

Over the centuries, the arts of piecing, ap-pliquéing, and quilting have flourished in different parts of the world at different times. With the possible exception of quilting (which is virtually ignored in many warm climates) some form of all of these needlework techniques exists in most countries. It is the aim of this book to focus only on those indigenous forms of these crafts that are unique to their country of origin. The projects are intended as adaptations

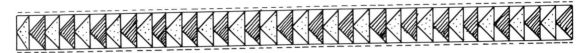

rather than authentic replicas of each craft. They are glimpses into other cultures and frequently adapted to the busy schedules of most modern quiltmakers.

Whether you are interested in working in the style of Japanese sashiko, Italian trapunto, English template patchwork, or one of the other crafts represented in this book, you will be using fundamental skills in piecing, appliquéing, or quilting. If you are a beginner, you will first need to feel comfortable with the basics. You will find that the easy projects in the chapter titled "America" provide a good starting point for building your needlework skills.

Notice that all of the projects offered in this book are labeled as to their level of difficulty. If your experience with sewing and quiltmaking is limited, try a few easy projects first. Resist the urge to jump right in. Read a project carefully to be sure you can visualize all of the steps you will be following.

The project instructions describe which materials and methods to use to complete a project exactly like the sample pictured. Don't let this detailed approach discourage your creativity, however. Do not feel limited to the few variations that are suggested for each project.

No one can tell you the "right" way to make a quilt or a quilted project. All they can tell you is what *their* way is. In these projects, the simplest and most authentic way has been selected for you, but do not be afraid to try your own variations based on your creative intuition. If your ideas fail to turn out quite as planned, they will still provide you with a valuable learning experience. As a beginning quilter, it might seem as if a perfectly finished project is your main goal. In time, you may come to find, as have many quilters, that the real benefits of quiltmaking lie in what it teaches us about ourselves—lessons about patience and ingenuity. Or, to paraphrase John Ruskin, the highest reward for our toil is not what we get for it, but what we become by it.

# A Good Start

Have all of your materials ready before you begin. Use quality fabrics and thread, anything less may fade or fall apart. The expenditure of your valuable time justifies the expense of quality materials. Always preshrink fabric just as you would if sewing clothing. Do this by washing the fabric by hand or in the washing machine. Remember to test for colorfastness while you're at it.

With projects that call for batting, remember that polyester batting is more forgiving. Cotton batting requires a little more effort in pushing the needle through and may shift somewhat if the project is ever washed. Quilts filled with wool should not be washed. Dry cleaning can ruin quilt stitches. Quilts should be washed as seldom as possible and materials for them chosen with an eye to this. Low loft and traditional quilt batting are easier to quilt through. You may choose high loft batting, however, if you want a high relief to your design.

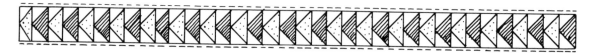

# Making Templates

All templates for projects can be found at the back of the book. To begin templates, trace each pattern onto tracing paper. From there, re-trace onto cardboard or sandpaper. Sandpaper templates, with the sandy side down, cling lightly to fabric, and are less likely to shift while you are using the template to mark fabric.

Quilting templates are drawn in this book with a single dotted line. Piecing and appliquéing templates have a double outline. We will discuss quilting templates later. With templates used for piecing, the inner template line is the sewing line. In templates for appliqué, this inner line indicates where a shape is to be folded or turned under to eliminate ragged edges. In templates used for piecing, the space between the inner and outer line is a seam allowance (Fig. 1-1). In appliqué templates, it is a margin for turning under. The outer line is the cutting line for both kinds of templates.

When making templates for piecing and appliquéing, you may want to make two templates for each pattern—one for the outer line and one for the inner line. This will give you an exact copy of the pattern in the book. Or, if you are experienced at template making, trace from the inner line only, and estimate for yourself as you mark and cut your fabric shapes, how much fabric you wish for a seam allowance/turning under margin.

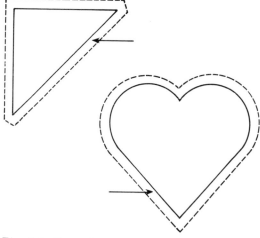

*Fig. 1-1. Example of seam allowance.*

# Marking and Cutting Fabric

Once your templates are made, use them to mark your fabric. Iron all of the fabric before you begin. Mark on the wrong side of the fabric. Trace around the outside of each template. If using two templates to mark both inner and outer template lines, do the large template first and center the smaller one inside it. Use a chalk pencil on dark fabrics, a soft lead pencil for marking light fabrics.

Follow the marked lines carefully when cutting out fabric shapes to ensure correct size. For appliqué shapes, you will need to clip all concave or in-turning curves. This will keep the outer edge of the appliqué

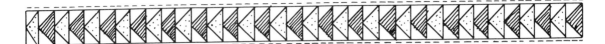

from stretching as it is turned under. The templates pictured for each project indicate where you will need to clip your appliqué shapes.

# Piecing

Once the shapes are cut out, you are ready to sew them together. Fabric shapes to be pieced are usually geometric in style and have straight edges, but the edges may be curved. Piecing is simply joining shapes, blocks, or borders in seams. It can be done by hand or on a sewing machine.

With a few stated exceptions, most of the projects in this book are adaptable to hand sewing or machine sewing. If you are more comfortable with a machine, you might want to review the suggestions for machine piecing and appliquéing that appear further on in this chapter.

Hand piecing is done with a running stitch—a simple up-and-down stitch that follows the sewing line marked on your fabric about 1/4" from the outer edge (Fig. 1-2).

Matching seams exactly is what gives pieced quilts their strong graphic appeal. The following "pin-through" method will aid you in lining up fabric shapes, and when joining groups of shapes, to achieve perfectly matched seams (Fig. 1-3). Hold two fabric shapes with right sides together. You will need to position the shapes so that the two pencil sewing lines on either shape are directly lined up. Put a straight pin through the pencil line facing you. Position the second fabric shape so that the pin goes

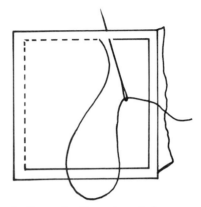

Fig. 1-2. Example of running stitch.

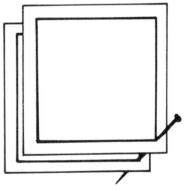

Fig. 1-3. Pin-through method.

through *its* pencil line on the side facing away from you. Do the same in several places along the sewing line of the fabric shapes. Don't bother to secure these pins. They are just for lining up, not for holding the two fabric shapes securely together. Now, using one or two more straight pins, securely pin the shapes together. Finally, remove the original pins used to line up the

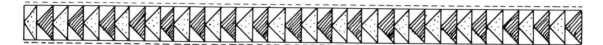

sewing lines. This will leave the pencil line free as a guide for sewing.

Use a running stitch to join the fabric shapes together. The color of thread need not match the fabric color exactly. Use dark thread for dark colored fabrics and light thread for light colors. Knot your thread and sew with a doubled or a single strand.

When you join the rows or groups of shapes to others, be sure to line up the sewn seams first. After you've assured yourself of having matched the seams correctly, go on to line up the shapes along the remainder of the sewing line.

Depending on the size of your project, you may want to iron the sewn groups of shapes more than once. Frequent ironing is one of the secrets of precise quilt piecing. Iron on the wrong side of the fabric. Do not iron the seams open as you would in making clothing. Press the seams of light-colored fabric toward the dark pieces of fabric next to them. Press dark seams toward dark fabric. Avoid, if you can, ironing dark seams toward light fabric. The seams will show through the light material, distracting the eye away from your design and reducing graphic appeal.

# Appliqué

Appliqué involves sewing patches of fabric onto another background fabric. After your marked fabric shapes are cut out, they must be clipped. Clip all inward-turning curves and corners up to, but not into, the fold line. This is the inner line marked on all appliqué templates in this book. Once the patches are clipped, they are ready to be appliquéd. When doing appliqué projects in this book, consult the photograph of the sample project for proper positioning. Read the project directions through ahead of time and be sure not to pin the shapes too close to the outer edge of the project. These edges will most likely be trimmed.

After the shapes have been pinned in place, they are ready to be appliquéd. Thread a "sharps" needle with thread that matches the appliqué fabric (not the background fabric) exactly. Make a knot in one end of the thread. Do not double the thread, but sew with a single strand. This will make your appliqué stitches almost invisible to the eye.

In appliqué, the stitches are hidden just under the edge of the fabric shape. Only a tiny portion of each stitch should show along the outer edge of the shape. Take close tiny stitches on the right side of your project, about ⅛" apart. The stitches on the wrong side of the project may be farther apart, ¼" or so. Bring the thread up from the back of the project and directly through the fold in the appliqué shape. Then run the thread back down into the background fabric. As you sew, turn under the raw edge of the appliqué shape.

If you are working on an especially intricate shape, and find you are having trouble, you may decide to try pre-basting your shapes. In this case, baste the edges of your appliqué shapes under before you even pin them in place. Use basting thread in a color

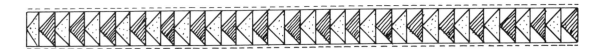

*Fig. 1-4. Appliqué summer bedspread, Indian cotton print, c.1810. Photograph courtesy of Stamford Historical Society.*

that contrasts with your appliqué to allow for easy removal later. Once the shapes are appliquéd and secure, remove the basting stitches. This method is more time-consuming, but it may be useful if you find yourself having difficulty with turning the shapes under accurately as you go.

When you have finished the appliqué, you may want to iron your work. Press from the wrong side of the fabric and iron only

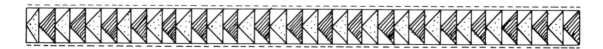

*Fig. 1-5. Detail of Fig. 1-4.*

the background fabric, not the appliqué shapes themselves. This will allow them to keep a slightly puffy, textured look.

# Setting Blocks

In a block quilt or project, sewing the quilt blocks together is called "setting" the blocks. The blocks themselves may have been pieced or appliquéd, but they should be sewn together using the proper piecing techniques to ensure matched seams along the blocks. Before setting, lay out all of the blocks just as they will appear in the finished quilt or project. Join them together in pairs and then join the pairs. Some people

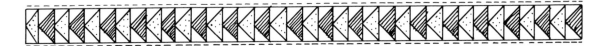

find that joining blocks in clusters is easier than joining strips of squares. When all of the blocks have been joined together, iron the finished piece.

# Quilting

Quilting means sewing together three fiber layers—usually a decorated top fabric, a middle layer of batting, and a bottom fabric layer. The quilting is the stitching that holds these three layers together, making them appear as one single fabric layer.

The first step in preparing the individual layers for quilting is to put the bottom fabric right side down on a large work surface (a clean floor will often do). Using masking tape, tape the bottom layer directly onto the work surface so it won't shift. Next, the batting is arranged over this with at least a 2″ overlap all the way around beyond the edge of the bottom fabric. Finally the decorated fabric is placed right side up on top of these. The top and bottom fabric layers should line up; the batting should extend beyond both at least 2″.

Baste the three layers together or use small non-rusting brass safety pins to pin them together. Lines of basting should be fairly close, 4″ to 6″ apart. Basting should run not only up and down but from side to side as well. If you use pins, leave no more than a 4″ to 6″ square space unpinned. Close basting will ensure that your quilt behaves like one layer of fabric rather than three when you are handling it.

A chalk pencil or chalk wheel works

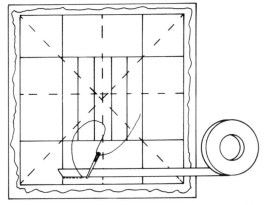

*Fig. 1-6. Avoid marking by using quilter's masking tape.*

best for marking most quilt fabrics. The marked lines come out with ease and the chalk can be purchased in colors that will stand out sufficiently on the fabric. Take care in using water soluable markers. They don't always wash out as expected and certain chemicals can turn them brown.

Marking can be avoided altogether in straight line quilting by using removable quilter's ¼″ masking tape and removing it as a line of quilting is sewn (Fig. 1-6). Or, a project may call for the use of a quilting template. Most of the quilting templates in this book can be cut from paper and pinned directly on the quilt so that a line of quilting may be run all the way around the outside and the template removed. The template serves as a guide for your stitches (Fig. 1-7).

The quilting templates offered here have a single dotted outline unlike the piecing and appliquéing templates which have a double outline. Quilting templates should

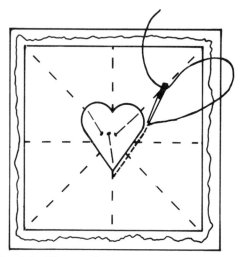

Fig. 1-7. *The template serves as a guide for your stitches.*

be photocopied or traced onto regular bond paper and cut out on the outline. You may want to make more than one copy depending on how many times in the project the template is to be used. A simple paper template will usually hold up after being used four to six times.

Plan to quilt ¼″ inside pieced geometric shapes. Quilt ¼″ outside appliqué shapes. Other quilting variations include contour quilting and quilting-in-the-ditch. Contour quilting is especially useful in landscape appliqué. Repeated lines of quilting create an impression of textured hills and ridges. Quilting in the ditch is running a line of quilting just inside the seams of your pieced work. It is usually more difficult than quilting across fabric areas. Avoid as much as possible quilting over seam allowances.

Large projects may be quilted in a hoop or a frame, small ones in a hoop. If using a frame, attach the sides of the quilt to the side bars of the frame. The frame should hold the quilt taut but not tight—that is, it should not pull or stretch the layers. To quilt from the center (as is preferred), roll both sides of the quilt on the frame.

Quilting hoops come in many sizes from 14″ to 24″ and larger. To use a hoop, place the fixed circle of the hoop on the work surface, the center part of the quilt over it, and adjust the moveable circle over the fixed one. The material should not be stretched taut but should have some give to it. Begin your quilting in the middle of the hoop, rather than at one side (Fig. 1-8).

To sew quilting stitches, you need betweens quilting needles which are shorter than regular sharps. The shorter your needle, the tinier and finer your quilting stitch will be. Change quilting needles fairly often. A needle has become dull when the

Fig. 1-8. *Quilting using a hoop.*

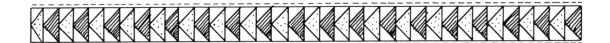

shine wears off and it has turned steely gray. A dull, discolored needle is harder to push through the fabric. Unless you change needles regularly, you'll find yourself having a vague sense of dissatisfaction with what should be an enjoyable task. When your needle finally breaks or becomes too dull to push through the fabric, you will be forced to change anyway.

Use a thimble. Even if it feels funny at first, give yourself time to get used to it. With practice, it can make a big difference in your comfort, stitching, and enjoyment of quilting large projects. If a thimble is hard to get used to, get yourself a special one. A thimble that belonged to a loved relative, reminds you of a special place, or even an antique one that pleases you can help you overcome the initial antipathy which almost everyone experiences. Then, challenge yourself to wear it a little each day, even if you do not quilt every day. In time, you will probably wonder how you ever sewed without it.

To begin quilting, use one strand of quilting thread in your needle. Make a small knot at the end of the thread. You will work with one hand (your right hand, if you are right-handed) on the top of the quilt and one hand below it. Insert the needle through the top and batting of the project, and back out the top. Pull the thread sharply so that the knot goes through the top fabric layer and loses itself in the batting.

Wear a metal thimble on the middle finger of the hand on top of the quilt. With the eye of the needle against the thimble,

position the needle so that it enters the quilt from the top at an angle. One finger of your hand underneath the quilt should make gentle contact with the needle. To prevent soreness on this finger, tape a small bit of adhesive tape over the fingertip or allow a callous to form. (Stringed instrument players have an easy time of quilting, having already acquired calloused fingertips!)

Use the finger on the "underneath" hand to put pressure on the quilt from the bottom. As this finger presses a slight ridge in the quilt from underneath, the point of the needle is guided back up to the quilt's surface. Push the needle through the layers with pressure from the hand on top. Pull the needle and thread through to make a single stitch. Begin by taking single running stitches like this in a line of quilting. Be sure to go through all three layers of the quilt with each stitch. When you feel comfortable with the single stitch, begin "loading" the needle, first with two stitches at a time; later, with more. Eventually, you should be able to develop a "rocking" motion with your needle that allows you to take several stitches at once.

Rotate the project so you are quilting in a direction that is comfortable for you. Quilt stitches should be as tiny as you can make them. Consistency in stitches, however, is more important than size. It is fine to take as few as five stitches to the inch as long as all five stitches are the same length. Ideally, an inch of quilting should contain between six and nine stitches. (Antique quilts may have as many as fifteen to the inch.) No more

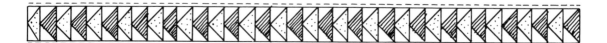

than four to six square inches of quilt should be left unquilted, even less if you opt for cotton batting. To finish a line of thread, take two or more backstitches, run the thread through the batting for an inch or so and cut. Do not make a final knot.

# Binding

To bind a quilt or wall hanging, you will need to cut strips of fabric that coordinate with your project. Usually the strips should be cut no more than 2″ wide. (You may want to use a rotary cutter for cutting strips.) Binding is folded and turned over the raw edge of a project so it always finishes to be one quarter of the width of the actual fabric strip used to make it. For instance, a binding strip 2″ in width will yield a ½″ wide binding.

Once the strips are cut, they are folded down the center and ironed. The folded or doubled strips are then machine sewn with a ½″ seam to the quilt front. A doubled binding strip is sewn to each side of the quilt edge with the ragged edges of the quilt and the binding all lined up evenly.

At each corner, the binding of one side is lined up flat against the binding from the nearest side. This involves folding or manipulating the quilt slightly. A sewing line in the shape of an upside down V joins the two binding lengths. The V should extend about ¾″ from tip to point with one tip falling at the corner where the two binding lengths meet, the point falling at the middle

of the binding (width-wise), and the remaining tip falling at a point exactly opposite that first corner. When all four binding corners are sewn, the excess binding may be trimmed to within ⅜″ of the V-shaped sewing line. The doubled binding is then folded over and around the ragged edge of the quilt creating a perfectly mitered corner. The binding is sewn down by hand on the back with a hem or appliqué stitch.

# Machine Sewing

Most of the projects in this book can be pieced or appliquéd by hand or by machine. The quilted projects call for hand quilting. In at least one case, that of Seminole patchwork, use of a sewing machine is essential. The technique of cutting sewn patches in Seminole work demands the extra-strong stitching provided by a machine.

If you are a beginner at doing patchwork, it will probably be best to start out with hand sewing. Matching seams, making perfect patchwork points, and setting corners are all easier done by hand. The value of machine work, of course, is that it is much faster and stronger than hand sewing. If you are confident about your ability to handle a machine, there is no reason not to tackle the projects in this way. The following suggestions are intended as a review for experienced machine sewers. If you are a beginner and feel strongly about doing the projects by machine, obtain one or more books on machine piecing and appliquéing from your local library.

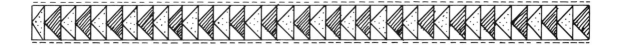

*Fig. 1-9. "The Dunes." Hand appliquéed wall hanging quilted by the author.*

# Machine Piecing

Set the machine at 10–12 stitches per inch. With your fabric shapes marked and cut out, pin fabric pieces together with right sides together. (See the description of the "pin-through" method described earlier.) Insert the edge of the two shapes under the presser foot and begin sewing. Use a straight stitch. Remove pins just before you come to them.

Use no more than a ¼″ seam allowance in machine piecing. Some presser feet are exactly ¼″ wide. Such a presser foot can be used as a sewing guide. If this is not the case with your machine, mark the throat plate with masking tape so that you have a ¼″ guide mark as you sew. Backstitch at the beginning and end of each line of sewing. Clip threads as each pair or group of fabric shapes is removed. Use a seam ripper to remove any unwanted stitches. Turn the piece over and remove threads from the

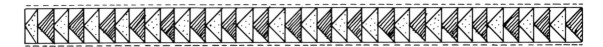

wrong side of the fabric. Iron joined patches before sewing them to other joined patches.

# Machine Appliquéing

By hand or machine, loosely baste under the 1/4″ outer edge of each appliqué shape. Use basting thread in a color that contrasts with the appliqué to allow for easy removal later.

When the edges are turned under, pin or tack the shapes in place on the back-ground fabric. Use a straight stitch or decorative zigzag stitch to sew them securely. Pull the threads to the back of the piece when beginning and ending and tie by hand, rather than using a back stitch to secure your work.

If you prefer, you can use a satin stitch to appliqué shapes. This eliminates basting. The shapes are cut on the inner template line, rather than the outer line. Then the raw edges are hidden by a band of satin stitch sewing all around the outside of the appliqué shape.

# Part One: NORTH AMERICA

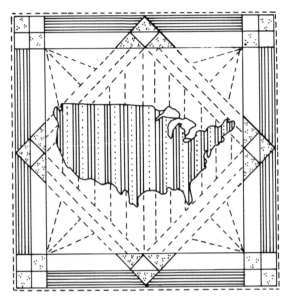

# Chapter Two | America: Piecing & Appliquéing

# A BRIEF HISTORY OF QUILTING IN AMERICA

The hardships endured by early American colonists can scarcely be appreciated today. By our own standards, the lifestyle that many settlers left behind in Europe was difficult enough. On the shores of the New World, they constantly had to adapt and re-learn hard lessons—what plants could be eaten with safety, what herbs provided healing, how to survive against hunger and disease, and how to make do with the tools they had brought with them.

While most men enjoyed some respite in outdoor chores like farming, hunting, and fishing, women often found themselves confined to dark, stuffy, windowless cabins raising children, cooking, cleaning, spinning and sewing. Looking back upon her arrival in the New World, American poet Anne Bradstreet wrote: "After a short time I changed my condition and was married, and came into this country, where I found a new world and new manners, at which my heart rose. But after I was convinced it was the way of God, I submitted to it. . ."[1]

The earliest surviving records of women's attitudes toward the vast wilderness typically reflect a grim attitude. That these early pioneers and subsequent generations of frontier women turned to colorful quilt-making as a creative and meditative outlet is hardly surprising.

From the days of the first settlers, no quilts remain. Whether this is because quilts that existed wore out or because they were not used in the first place is unclear. It is quite possible that the early settlers brought quilts with them, but once here, the rigors of daily life may have precluded quiltmaking. Mere survival was at stake and bedcovers made of furs, though difficult to clean, were readily available. Homemade linen and wool took an astonishing amount of time to produce—as much as 16 months from planting to final processing in the case of flax.[2] As life became a little easier more women turned to quilting to satisfy practical needs as well as personal creativity.

We like to think of our forebears as having lived life at a slower pace. But the exigencies of surviving in a hostile environment made them time-conscious in their own way. American quilters came to use the faster, less thread-wasteful running stitch rather than the backstitch commonly used back home in England.

The first record of quilts in America appear in wills and inventories of the late 1600s. About this time, we can surmise that the fabrics and colors used in quilts were those used in dress. The kind and quality of these depended largely on location. A New England Puritan woman would likely have

worn sturdy homespun in rich earthy colors: dark green, crimson, russet, tan. The wife of a wealthy southern planter might have dressed in brocade, lace, velvet, cambric, dimity, or calico. Dutch colonists enjoyed silks, velvets and fine linens. In particular, Dutch needlewomen perpetuated a tradition from their homeland of making and wearing quilted garments.

A family's proximity to a seaport also determined the kinds of fabrics used. Some fancy foreign cloth made its way into colonial towns, although frontier settlers would have relied on their own homespun for quilts and clothing.

Probably the earliest surviving American quilt is the Saltonstall Quilt believed to have been made about 1704. It features an elaborate pattern of squares and triangles using English-style paper templates. About this time, references to quilts regularly appeared in wills and inventories. Newspaper advertisements offered quilts, quilted clothing, and lessons in quiltmaking.

In an age of high birth rate and high mortality, the bed was an important item of furniture in the home and even a mark of wealth. It was commonly kept in the parlor or living room on the first floor of the house and provided an excuse for creative sewing skills to be shown to advantage.

During the first half of the 18th century, life for colonial Americans grew increasingly more stable. A wider diversity of goods, including fabrics, was available from other parts of the world. The demands made by England upon her American colonies, however, would soon bring vast changes.

The seeds of revolution had been sown as early as 1650 with the passing of the Navigation Act which sought to restrict colonial trade to English goods from English ships. Clothmaking was restricted. Textile machines and skilled workers could not be sent to the colonies from England. By the mid-1700s, the colonists were being subjected to a wide variety of hated laws and taxes. American settlers retaliated by boycotting English goods and it became a symbol of patriotism to use homespun cloth in dress and needlework.

The lifting of the trade embargo following the War of 1812 put an end to such restrictions. By the early 1800s, a wide variety of imported and domestic fabric was available to most quilters. The result was an unprecedented creative outpouring that has come to be regarded as "the flowering of American quiltmaking."

Quilting became popular with women from all walks of life. It provided women in rural areas with a social framework in sewing circles and quilting bees. It gave wealthy, leisured women a chance to show off highly-developed needle skills and luxurious fabrics. It offered all women what was routinely denied to them in a society that revolved around the ideals and activities of men—self-expression, self-esteem, and personal identity.

Quilting skills had been brought to this country by Europeans, but as Jonathan Holstein observed, "the great development of

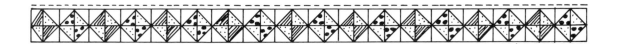

*Fig. 2-1. Detail of appliqué quilt by Harriet Knapp, dated 1854. Photograph courtesy of Stamford Historical Society.*

quilt design, especially that type which uses repetitive figures building to an overall effect, was distinctly American."[3]

In America, the block setting for quilts became predominant.[4] Block patterns were easy to pick up and put down. They did not require a large unused space in which to organize an all-over pattern. They were easy to work with and traveled well. After all, our "mobile society" was already on the move, constantly pressing on to new frontiers. Women created countless block patterns that reminded them of the things that touched their everyday lives: Ducks and Geese, The Schoolhouse, The Bear's Paw, The Pine Tree. The westward migration

alone inspired such pattern names as Rocky Road to Kansas, Prairie Star, and Wagon Tracks.

Near the end of the 19th century, quilt fashions changed. The crazy quilt came into vogue (discussed in Chapter Three). Scraps of velvet, silk, and satin were covered intensively with rich embroidery to create a design that was bursting with energy. By the turn of the century, however, the crazy quilt had lost its fashionable edge.

Quiltmaking itself lost popularity for a time, but experienced a revival during the Depression years. Perhaps it was the WPA, creating employment by stimulating craftwork that reawoke enthusiasm for quiltmaking; perhaps the need for thrift and self-reliance. In any case, the art was revitalized.

The 1970s also brought forth a burst of quiltmaking energy in America and abroad. Recent interest in quilts has been fueled by their recognition as a viable art form. In part that recognition has come about as the result of an important exhibit first held at the Whitney Museum of Art in 1971, titled "Abstract Design in American Quilts" and organized by Jonathan Holstein. It made the revolutionary step of showing quilts in a museum setting, giving them an aesthetic recognition they had never before enjoyed. Where quilters had thought of their work as a pastime, they began to see it as an art form and themselves as fabric artists. As Holstein himself observed, "We can see in many [quilts], such phenomena as 'op' effects, serial images, use of 'color fields,' a deep understanding of negative space, man-

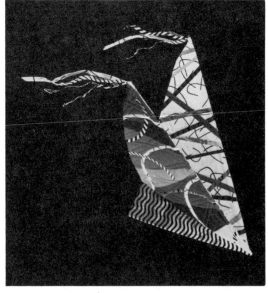

Fig. 2-2. "Cast Your Fate to the Wind." Quilted kite by fabric artist Linda Behar. Exhibited in the 21st Annual Celebration of American Crafts at Creative Arts Workshop in New Haven, CT. Photograph by David Caras, courtesy of the artist.

nerisms of formal abstraction. . ." and other elements of contemporary painting.[5]

Today, as more women enter the profession of fine arts, the unique tactile qualities of fiber art are being fully explored. If quilters have had an influence on the art world, the reverse is also true. Many quilters who once found abstract art inaccessible can relate to the floating squares of painter Josef Albers. Others see similarities between their abstract piecing and the canvases of Cubist painters. At home and abroad, needlewomen and fiber artists are joining forces to steer the art of quilting into exciting, uncharted waters.

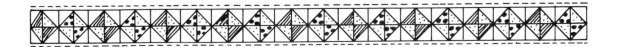

## NOTES

1. Sylvia R. Frey and Marian J. Morton, *New World, New Roles: A Documentary History of Women in Pre-Industrial America* (Westport, CT: Greenwood Press, 1986), p. 68.

2. Patsy and Myron Orlofsky, *Quilts in America* (New York: McGraw Hill, 1974), p. 11.

3. Jonathan Holstein, *American Pieced Quilts* (New York: Viking Press, 1972), p. 11.

4. Barbara Brackman, "The Strip Tradition in European-American Quilts," *The Clarion* (Fall 1989), p. 45.

5. Holstein, p. 34.

# TECHNIQUES OF PIECING AND APPLIQUÉING

*Fig. 2-3. Detail of pieced fans quilt, Vermont, c. 1930.*

In pieced work, fabric shapes (usually having one or more straight edges) are joined edge to edge to form geometric patterns. In appliqué, fabric shapes are turned under and sewn onto a background fabric. Typically the quilting of a pieced design is done

about ¼″ inside the pieced shapes. Or the quilting may be done in an all-over pattern that disregards the colored pattern of the top, such as straight line or clam shell quilting. Usually the quilting of an appliqué design is done about ¼″ outside each appliqué shape.

Sometime during the 19th century, piecing came to be regarded by many American quilters as the method of choice for constructing more utilitarian quilts. Gener-

ally, appliqué was reserved for fancy coverlets. That distinction no longer applies. Many of today's pieced quilts constitute quilted masterpieces and, although most quilters have a collection of fabric scraps lurking in a closet somewhere, few would rely on leftover scraps to create as time-consuming a project as a pieced quilt. In contemporary quiltmaking, piecing and appliquéing enjoy equal "status" and are often both featured in a single quilt.

# PIECED PILLOW

Difficulty Level: Easy

Please review Piecing and Quilting in the chapter on Basic Techniques before beginning. See completed project in color section (Plate 2).

This fairly easy project will give the beginning quilter a feel for the techniques used in traditional pieced work. The method of sewing the pillow backing from two pieces of fabric (instead of one) allows the pillow cover to be removed easily for cleaning.

### SUGGESTED VARIATIONS

Muslin with any favorite calico; light, medium, and dark progressive hues of same color for small, medium and large triangles to enhance "outward" movement of pattern.

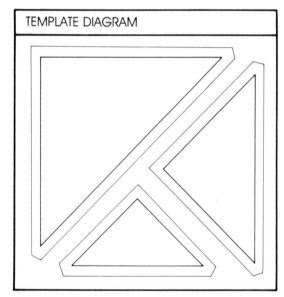

TEMPLATE DIAGRAM

*Templates for this project look like this and are found at the back of the book.*

*Fig. 2-4. Pieced Pillow project.*

## MATERIALS

¼ yard white or unbleached muslin
16″ × 16″ square muslin (quilt backing)
Two 10″ × 15″ rectangles muslin (pillow
    backing)
16″ × 16″ square batting
¼ yard light blue calico
14″ × 14″ square pillow form
White quilting thread

## DIRECTIONS

1. To make templates, photocopy or trace the patterns for the three different sizes of triangles: small, medium, and large. You will notice that the medium triangle is exactly the same size as two small triangles put side by side. The large triangle is the same size as two medium triangles put together. This is what gives the pattern a feeling of movement from the center outwards.

2. Use the templates you have made to mark and cut out 8 small white triangles, 8 small blue triangles; 4 medium white triangles, 4 medium blue triangles; 4 large white triangles, and 4 large blue triangles.

3. Lay out the cut fabric triangles to form the pattern. Refer to Fig. 2-5 and color Plate 2 of the project as needed. As you sew, keep in mind that the pattern is set up in such a way that two blue sides never touch, and two white sides never touch. This is what creates the contrast that makes this pattern "work." If you catch yourself sewing two blue sides together stop and reassess your sewing.

4. With right sides together, sew a small white triangle to a small blue one along one short side. This forms a triangle pair. With right sides together, sew the remaining small triangles in pairs. Matching seams as you go, sew the pairs together (right sides

together) to form the square central pattern. Use all of the small triangle pairs.

5. With right sides together, sew one medium white triangle to one medium blue triangle. Do the same for the remaining medium triangles. Matching seams, and with right sides together, sew the medium triangle pairs to the center square made up of small triangles. You have added to the center square, making it larger.

6. With right sides together, sew the large triangles into pairs just as you did the smaller ones. Matching seams, and with right sides together, sew the large triangle pairs to the new larger center square. Iron the sewn pieced pillow top.

7. On your work surface, place the 16″ square quilt backing right side down, then the batting, then the pillow top right side up. Pin together and baste.

8. Quilt ¼″ inside each triangle, using narrow quilter's masking tape as a guide to keep your lines of quilting straight.

9. Remove the basting threads. Trim the excess batting and quilt backing from the quilted pillow to make it even on all sides.

10. The two 10″ × 15″ muslin rectangles will form the back of the pillow. Lay out one rectangle on your work surface wrong side up and horizontally so that the longer sides of the rectangle are at the top and bottom.

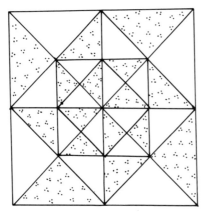

*Fig. 2-5. Piecing diagram for Pieced Pillow project.*

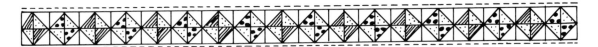

Fold one of the long sides under about ½" and then ½" again to hide the ragged edge. Pin this fold in place and sew, using a sewing machine or by hand, using a hem stitch. Do the same for the second rectangle.

11. Turn the rectangles over so they are right side up. Place the sewn edges over one another so that they overlap by at least 2". Adjust the overlap until the entire square made by the two rectangles measures 15" on each side. Pin the pillow backing to hold this shape and baste the two rectangles together along the overlap.

12. On the wrong side of the pillow top, mark a ½" seam allowance all around the inside of the square. The seam allowance line should mark out a 14" × 14" square. Do the same for the basted pillow backing, also on the wrong side of the fabric.

13. With right sides together, pin the pillow top to the basted pillow back. Sew the top to the backing on all four sides. Use a sewing machine or a close running stitch with an occasional back stitch, if sewing by hand.

14. Remove the basting from the pillow backing and turn the finished quilted pillow cover right side out. It is ready to be fitted over the 14" pillow form.

# PEACE QUILT

### Difficulty Level: Challenging

Please review Piecing and Quilting in the chapter on Basic Techniques before beginning. See completed project in color section (Plate 1).

Another name for the Double Wedding Ring is Friendship Ring. The interlocking circles of this design reflect a wish for peace as our world draws closer together through sharing and appreciation of cultural differences.

## SUGGESTED VARIATIONS

Bright, rich solids in place of the calicos. Note: the calicoes used in the original project all feature one color plus a tiny, subtle, black print. Multi-colored calicoes would make this already energetic pattern too busy.

## MATERIALS

1 yard each calico: lavender, magenta, blue, smoke green, aqua, purple, bright green
1½ yards red calico (patches and binding)
3 yards solid turquoise
¼ yard white (doves)
¼ yard medium green (land masses and olive branches)

*Templates for this project look like this and are found at the back of the book.*

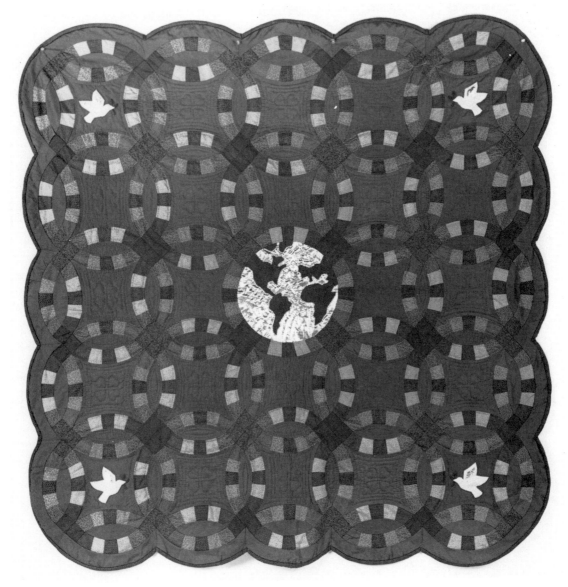

*Fig. 2-6. Peace Quilt project.*

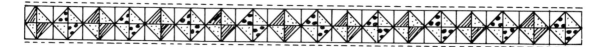

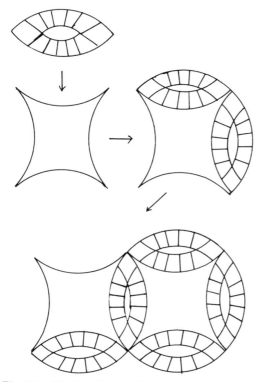

Fig. 2-7. *Piecing diagram for Peace Quilt project.*

scrap silver metallic fabric (wing decorations on doves)

2 spools Navy quilting thread

½ yard light blue glitz fabric (earth)

75″ × 75″ square of batting

75″ × 75″ square of backing fabric

## DIRECTIONS

1. This Wedding Ring features 25 interlocking circles or rings. The circles are made up of pieced ovals. The center circle, filled in by the earth motif, is made up of half ovals so it will be discussed separately. The remaining 24 circles consist of 56 ovals. Trace all templates onto cardboard and cut out.

2. Templates 1–4 are for the pieced ovals. Use them to mark and cut the following: template 1: 56 purple, 56 bright green; template 2: 112 blue; template 3: 112 aqua, 56

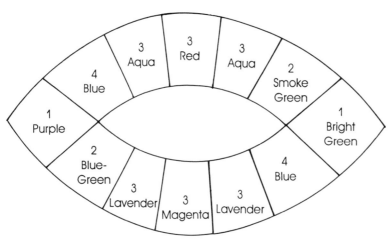

Fig. 2-8. *Piecing diagram for Peace Quilt project.*

red, 112 lavender, 56 magenta; template 4: 56 blue-green, 56 smoke green.

3. From the solid turquoise use templates 5, 6, and 7 to mark and cut 56 oval centers, 24 "windows" or ring centers, and 20 outer arcs.

4. Use the remaining templates to mark and cut out the doves, their shiny wing decorations, olive branches, earth and land masses.

5. For the center ring cut the following additional patches: template 1: 2 purple, 2 bright green; template 2: 4 blue; template 3: 4 aqua, 2 red, 4 lavender, 2 magenta; template 4: 2 blue-green, 2 smoke green.

6. Piece 56 complete ovals. Piece two of each color half-oval for the center ring. (See piecing diagrams Figs. 2-7 and 2-8.)

7. Join the ovals to windows to make the interlocking rings. When you arrive at the center ring, join the half-ovals to make a circle of patches with an open center. Piece the blue glitz fabric earth into the center. If your glitz fabric is flimsy, you may want to baste it first to muslin before sewing in place. Continue to join the remaining ovals to complete all of the interlocking rings.

8. Join the outer arcs to the outer ring edges

to make a turquoise border all the way around the quilt.

9. Pin and appliqué in place the doves, their wing decorations, olive branches, and the land masses.

10. Place the quilt backing on a clean floor and tape the edges to keep it from shifting. Lay the batting over this and the pieced and appliquéd quilt top on the batting right side up. Baste the three layers together.

11. Quilt the pieced sections of the project, using the window template cut from paper and pinned in place. Quilt stitches are run just inside the outline of each heart cut out of the template. Then, run three lines of contour quilting from the window edges to the quilted hearts, using the window edges as a guide and marking with a chalk wheel before stitching. Quilt ¼" inside each pieced arc side of each oval and run a double line of contour quilting inside the center of each oval.

12. Quilt ¼" around the outside of the appliquéd sections of the project. Add lines of contour quilting in "waves" from the land masses to the outside perimeter of the earth. Remove basting threads.

13. Trim excess batting and backing fabric. Bind the project using 2" wide joined strips of red calico.

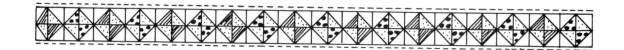

# HOMESPUN HEARTS WALL HANGING Difficulty Level: Easy

Please review Appliqué, Setting Blocks, and Quilting in the chapter on Basic Techniques before beginning. See completed project in color section (Plate 2).

**SUGGESTED VARIATIONS**

Calico instead of homespun for hearts; dark, rich, Amish-style solid colors for hearts, black squares instead of muslin.

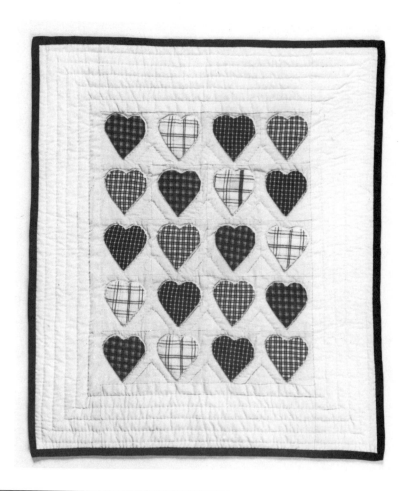

*Fig. 2-9. Homespun Hearts Wall Hanging project.*

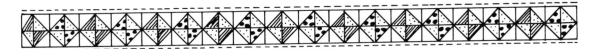

## TEMPLATE DIAGRAM

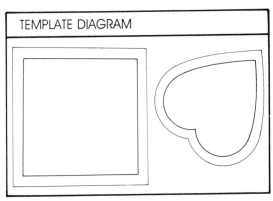

*Templates for this project look like this and are found at the back of the book.*

## MATERIALS

1 yard muslin for 20 blocks plus strips listed below
Two 4″ × 23″ muslin border strips
Two 4″ × 12″ muslin border strips
24″ × 27″ rectangle muslin backing
24″ × 27″ rectangle batting
⅛ yard each homespun fabrics in the following colors: red, green, red-and-blue, blue
Four 1½″ × 27″ strips solid navy blue binding
White quilting thread

## DIRECTIONS

1. To make templates, photocopy or trace the patterns for the hearts and blocks.

2. Use the heart template to mark and cut 5 hearts from each color of homespun. Use the block template to mark and cut 20 blocks from the muslin.

3. Using thread to match the homespun, turn under each heart appliqué, center, and sew onto a muslin block.

4. Lay out the heart blocks to form the pattern of the wall hanging.

5. Using the project sample as a guide, and with right sides together, sew together two adjacent blocks in the top row. In the same way, add on the remaining blocks to finish the top row. Sew each remaining row separately. Then, matching seams, and with right sides together, join the rows to form a large rectangle of heart blocks.

6. With right sides together, join the two long border strips along the long side of the pieced heart block rectangle. Join the two short border strips at the top and bottom. Iron the pieced and appliquéd heart design.

7. On your work surface, place the backing fabric right side down, then the batting, and place the heart design on top right side up. Pin and baste.

8. Quilt the project. Quilt ⅛″ around the outside of each heart. Quilt the border in lines of quilting 1″ apart, using quilter's

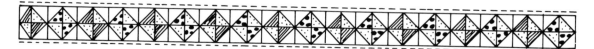

masking tape as a guide to ensure straight lines.

9. Remove the basting threads. Trim the excess batting and backing.

10. Bind the project using joined solid navy blue fabric strips. Add loops at the top for hanging the project if desired.

# APPLIQUÉ ROSE WREATH PILLOW Difficulty Level: Easy to Moderate

Please review Appliqué and Quilting in the chapter on Basic Techniques before beginning. See completed project in color section (Plate 2).

The Rose or Bridal Wreath was a favorite sampler block for friendship style wedding quilts. In this version, the wreath circle is broken into three slightly curving stems with their ends hidden under the flowers—much easier than sewing an actual circle.

## SUGGESTED VARIATIONS

Different colors for roses, darker greens for leaves, solid pastel instead of muslin.

## MATERIALS

6″ square solid pink (rose)
6″ square rose calico (rose)
6″ square maroon calico (rose)
6″ square solid yellow (rose center)
⅛ yard green calico (wreath stem, leaves and half-leaves)
⅛ yard solid green (leaves)

15″ × 15″ square muslin (background)
16″ × 16″ square muslin (quilt back)
Two 10″ × 15″ rectangles muslin (pillow backing)

TEMPLATE DIAGRAM

*Templates for this project look like this and are found at the back of the book.*

*Fig. 2-10. Appliqué Rose Wreath Pillow project.*

16″ × 16″ square batting
14″ × 14″ pillow form
White quilting thread

## DIRECTIONS

1. To make templates, photocopy or trace the patterns for the rose, leaf, half-leaf, rose center, and wreath stem. You will notice that the ends of the wreath stem and half-leaf do not have seam allowance. This is because these ends are hidden under other parts of the design.

2. Use the templates to mark and cut the fabric shapes: one rose each from solid pink, pink calico, and maroon calico; 6 leaves from solid green; 6 leaves, 6 half leaves and 3 wreath stems from green calico; and three rose centers from yellow.

3. Position the wreath stem to form a circle on the muslin background square, using color Plate 2 of the project as a guide. There should be about a 2″ space between the end of one stem and the beginning of the next. The roses will go over this space, so it will

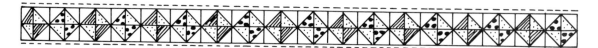

be hidden. Using thread to match the stem, appliqué in place.

4. Using matching thread, turn under a small portion of each rose, about ¼" along one edge. Tuck the base of a half-leaf under this sewn-under section of each rose and appliqué the rose edge on top of the half-leaf. Position each rose/half-leaf shape so as to cover the spaces in the wreath stem on the background square. Using thread to match the appliqué, sew in place.

5. Pin the leaves in place, using color Plate 2 as a guide. Turn under and appliqué in place.

6. Appliqué a rose center in the middle of each rose. Iron the appliquéd pillow top.

7. On your work surface, place the 16" square quilt backing right side down, then the batting, then the pillow top right side up. Pin together and baste.

8. Quilt ¼" around the outside of each shape. Use the small heart template to quilt a heart in the center of the wreath.

9. Remove the basting threads. Trim the excess batting and backing to make it even on all sides.

10. The two 10" × 15" muslin rectangles will form the back of the pillow. Lay out one rectangle on your work surface wrong side up and horizontally so that the longer sides of the rectangle are at the top and bottom. Fold one of the long sides under about ½" and then ½" again to hide the ragged edge. Pin this fold in place and sew using a sewing machine, or by hand using a hem stitch. Do the same for the second rectangle.

11. Turn the rectangles over so they are right side up. Place the sewn edges over one another so that they overlap by at least 2". Adjust the overlap until the entire square made by the two rectangles measures 15" on each side. Pin the pillow backing to hold this shape and baste the two rectangles together along the overlap.

12. On the wrong side of the pillow top, mark a ½" seam allowance all around the inside of the square. The seam allowance line should mark out a 14" × 14" square. Do the same for the basted pillow backing, also on the wrong side of the fabric.

13. With right sides together, pin the pillow top to the basted pillow back. Sew the top to the backing on all four sides. Use a sewing machine or a close running stitch with an occasionally back stitch if sewing by hand.

14. Remove the basting from the pillow backing and turn the finished quilted pillow cover right side out. It is ready to be fitted over the 14" pillow form.

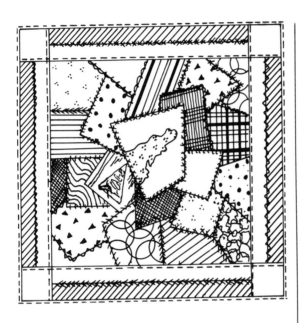

# Chapter Three

# New England: Crazy Patchwork

# THOSE CRAZY VICTORIANS

The Mark Twain Memorial in Hartford, Connecticut is a charming and lavish Victorian setting—the perfect starting point for a consideration of crazy patchwork, an indigenous American needlework style of the late 1800s.[1]

In this engaging house filled with nooks and crannies, Twain wrote, among other things, *Tom Sawyer* and *Huckleberry Finn*. He, his wife Livy, and their three daughters lived in grand style, entertaining important visitors. Filled with books, the library was the scene of family gatherings. Twain once recalled: "On these shelves, and on the mantelpiece, stood various ornaments. . . Every now and then the children required me to construct a romance—always impromptu—not a moment's preparation permitted—and into that romance I had to get all that bric-a-brac. . ."[2]

Twain's home, with its gables and turrets outside and select furniture and decorations by Louis Comfort Tiffany inside, reflected the height of Victorian fashion (Fig. 3-1). It would have been unthinkable for his family not to have had some items of crazy patchwork and they are, indeed, known to have owned at least one crazy quilt.[3]

Today, we seldom think of quilts as "fads." Quilts are usually appreciated for their traditional, enduring quality. Crazy quilts, however, arrived on the quiltmaking scene and disappeared almost as quickly.

Their tenure of stylishness was as brief as that of any modern rock musician. During the last quarter of the 19th century, they enjoyed immense popularity and then quietly faded away. They would not reappear until our own day when interest in all forms of folk art and needlecraft have been revived.

Just what constituted a crazy quilt? According to a set of pattern instructions from 1897: "Crazy patchwork has now become so popular as to require but little instruction. As the name indicates, it is simply sewing together odd pieces of silk, satin, plush, etc., in a way so that the angles may somewhat imitate the craze or crackle of old china, from which all this kind of work derives its name. The ornamenting of the seams with fancy stitches in bright-colored silks gives a very pleasing effect. . . Of course, no directions can be given as to the colors to be used, as this is where the taste of the worker is displayed."[4]

Crazy quilt fabric scraps were sewn onto a foundation fabric which was usually in the shape of a block. The blocks were joined and set with a rich plush or velvet border.

With its velvet and brocade, crazy patchwork was too heavy to quilt through. Instead it was usually tied or tacked to a fabric backing without a middle layer of padding. Only in very rare instances were Victorian-style silk and velvet crazy quilts

*Fig. 3-1. Antique photo showing the library and conservatory of the Mark Twain Memorial, Hartford, Connecticut, c.1890. Photograph courtesy of The Mark Twain Memorial.*

padded or quilted. Some crazy quilts, however, that appeared after the turn of the century were made of wool or cotton patches and occasionally had a middle layer and quilting.

Paradoxically, the ornate crazy design may have had its roots in traditional Japa-nese art which is noted for its simplicity. Crazy patchwork was even occasionally referred to as Japanese patchwork.[5] A kind of Japanese fabric patching known as *yosegire* may well have inspired American crazy patchwork. (We will explore this in a later chapter on Japan.)

Commodore Matthew Perry had forced Japan to relinquish its isolationist policies in 1853. From this time, Japanese painting, decorative arts, and decor quickly became the rage among fashionable westerners.[6] At the Centennial Exposition held in Philadelphia in 1876, the Japanese Pavillion was extremely popular. American enthusiasm was translated into needlework as well as clothing fashions, fabrics, home decorations, and wallpaper.

Crazy quilts appealed to people for many reasons. They provided a useful article from worthless silk scraps. They also constituted something of a social endeavor since women often exchanged bits of silk

*Fig. 3-2. Threads and antique silk cigarette premiums. Printed silk scraps such as these were eagerly sought after by women making crazy quilts.*

and ribbons. Even husbands and brothers could contribute by purchasing brands of cigarettes that came with colorful printed silks as a buying incentive (Fig. 3-2).

Crazy patchwork was used not just for bed coverings but as throws for lounges and daybeds, covers for tabletops, lambrequins (valances) for mantles, shelves, and windows, piano covers, even workbags and bookcovers were decorated with crazy patchwork.

In addition to fancy seam stitching, many crazy quilts featured embroidered pictures in the centers of patches. These included Kate Greenaway children, dogs, cats, birds, fans, cattails, sunflowers, roses, beetles, spiders, the moon and stars. More so during Victorian times than today, flowers were appreciated for their symbolism as well

as their pleasing form. To a typical Victorian lady, a rose stitched into a crazy quilt would have signified love. Daisies stood for innocence, pansies for remembrance, and a weeping willow branch for mourning.

Especially interesting among 19th century crazy quilt embroideries were pictures of spiders, flies, beetles, and other insects. Perhaps spiders' bug-catching qualities were more greatly appreciated in the days before screens and insecticide. Certainly their orb-shaped webs provided needlewomen with an appealing threadwork design. From a symbolic standpoint, the lowly spider also represented the kind of patience that was required to complete as complex a project as an elaborate crazy quilt.

Other bugs found their way into crazy patchwork as well. One writer in *Godey's*

*Fig. 3-3. Detail of appliquéed cotton crazy quilt from Vermont, c.1890. From the Shelburne Museum collection.*

*Ladies' Book* gushed over the common housefly as "the fancy ornament of the day; a pretty little fly. . ."[7] Perhaps our antiseptic age precludes us from rhapsodizing over insects, but there is something to be said for accepting beauty where we find it. The makers of crazy quilts looked around them and transcribed their everyday world in rich brilliant hues of silken thread.

In time, the more fashionable needleworkers abandoned the crazy quilt in favor of other forms of needlecraft. The crazy quilt evolved from a dainty silk throw to a more practical bed covering often made of wool or cotton. This more humble style of crazy quilt remained popular into the 1930s.[8]

Many Victorian crazy quilts which have survived into our own time present a prob-

*Fig. 3-4. Detail of star pattern in crazy quilt of silk, velvet, and brocade. Made by a member of the Cruikshank family, c. 1890. From the Stamford Historical Society collection.*

lem. They may not be around for much longer. The materials from which crazy quilts were made carry the seeds of their own destruction. Silk rots all by itself. The mordants with which most dye for antique silk was fixed contained metal salts which have increased the breakdown of the fibers. (It is a sobering thought! What mistakes are modern quilters making that textile experts 200 years from now will shake their heads over?)

In the recent past, people have tended to downplay the visual excitement of crazy quilts in favor of pieced and appliquéd quilts. The bold, geometric symmetry that is found in many pieced and repeating block designs is more in keeping with our culture's current aesthetic. Jonathan Holstein, for instance, condemns crazy patchwork as "cluttered" and "incoherent." One can almost imagine his voice rise in agitation as he cites further objections: "It was not meant for practical use; the work is fragile, as are the materials; it is difficult to clean. It is practically useless as a cover and impossible as design, and it took hundreds of hours to make."[9] Even quiltmaker Sue Bender in her insightful book *Plain and Simple* takes a potshot at crazy quilts when she likens her frantic lifestyle to one, in contrast to the calm intensity of Amish living and Amish colors.[10]

Fortunately, everyone is not quite so down on crazy patchwork. Many quiltmakers today appreciate the crazy patchwork style for its lively exuberance as well as the

chance it offers to use what have become offbeat fabrics in a challenging way. Quilt collectors appreciate heirloom crazy quilts for the things found in any kind of folk art—color, innocent use of design, and the touch of the maker's hand.

## NOTES

1. Penny McMorris, *Crazy Quilts* (New York: E.P. Dutton, Inc., 1984), p. 21.

2. Promotional material, The Mark Twain Memorial, 351 Farmington Avenue, Hartford, CT 06105.

3. Conversation with Maryann Curling, curator, Mark Twain Memorial.

4. McMorris, p. 32.

5. Ibid, p. 11.

6. Robert Rosenblum and H.W. Janson, *19th Century Art* (New York: Harry Abrams, Inc.), p. 289.

7. McMorris, p. 58.

8. Jeannette Lasansky, *Pieced by Mother* (Lewisburg, PA: An Oral Traditions Project of the Union Co. Historical Society), p. 86.

9. Jonathan Holstein, *The Pieced Quilt: An American Tradition* (Boston: Little, Brown, & Co., 1973), p. 62.

10. Sue Bender, *Plain and Simple: a Woman's Journey to the Amish* (San Francisco: Harper & Row, 1989), p. 4.

# TECHNIQUES OF CRAZY PATCHWORK

To begin, you will need a loosely woven foundation fabric. Any loosely woven muslin that is especially easy to sew through will work well. You will want to choose the kind of fabric that you would never use in doing cotton patchwork (since a loose weave frays easily in piecing and appliquéing.)

Your crazy patchwork shapes will look best if they are mostly cut with straight rather than curved edges, although an occa-

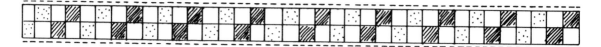

sional curved edge can be thrown in for variation. Use regular appliqué techniques for sewing down bits of satin, velvet or other fancy fabric patches. Japanese silk pins are especially useful in holding down turned-under patch edges until they can be sewn. (If your local quilt shop does not carry these, please see Supplies and Suppliers.) Do not turn under edges that are to be covered by other turned under edges. This saves time and also reduces bulkiness which is helpful when you begin to embroider the seams between patches. In choosing fabrics for patches, experiment with metallics and fabric that features unusual textures.

When all of the patches are sewn in place, embellish with embroidery. Use cotton or crewel embroidery floss and a large embroidery needle.

# HEART NECKLACE Difficulty Level: Easy

Please review Appliqué in the chapter on Basic Techniques before beginning. See completed project in color section (Plate 3).

This heart necklace will let you familiarize yourself with the techniques involved in crazy patchwork without a major expenditure of time. Best of all, when finished, it's fun to wear.

*Fig. 3-5. Heart Necklace project.*

## TEMPLATE DIAGRAM

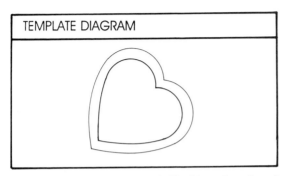

*Templates for this project look like this and are found at the back of the book.*

## MATERIALS

3″ × 3″ square muslin
3″ × 3″ square teal blue cotton
3″ × 3″ square traditional low-loft batting or fleece
Assorted colors of embroidery floss
Embroidery needle
Assorted solid color scraps of satin and/or silk
1 yard of satin soutache cording

## DIRECTIONS

1. Trace the heart template for this project. Mark and cut out one muslin heart and one teal heart.

2. Following the inner template line for the heart, mark and cut two hearts out of batting.

3. This project calls for covering only one side of the heart necklace with crazy patchwork. (You can, however, cover both if you like and have a reversible necklace.) To begin covering the muslin heart with patchwork, position and pin a small irregularly shaped scrap of satin or silk on the muslin heart. Pin a second scrap along one side of the first piece so one ragged edge of the first piece is hidden. With tiny appliqué stitches, turn under the side of the second scrap where it covers the first scrap.

4. Continue to add scraps until the muslin heart is covered. Be sure all ragged edges are turned under or covered by other scraps. Trim any excess scrap fabric which extends beyond the muslin heart.

5. Use decorative embroidery stitches along the edge of each scrap. Add beads, sequins, pearls, thin lace, or tiny embroidered decorations such as seed stitching, stars or flowers.

6. Center a small batting heart on the wrong side of the decorated muslin heart and pin. Baste the seam allowance of the decorated muslin heart over the edge of the batting heart, clipping as needed. Do the same with the undecorated teal heart.

7. Measure the cording to find where you want your heart to fall when it is worn. Cut the cording to the length you desire. Stitch the ends of the cording to the top of one heart, batting side up. Then with both batting sides facing in, pin the two hearts together. Whipstitch them together using em-

broidery floss. To finish off, add a tassel and a few strands of beaded floss to the heart point. This might be a good time to put any single unmatched earrings to use as further decoration either stitched on the heart front or added to the point.

# EMBROIDERED VEST  Difficulty Level: Easy to Moderate

Please review Appliqué and Binding in the chapter on Basic Techniques before beginning. See completed project in color section (Plate 3).

Recycling is not just for paper and aluminum. You can recycle an old vest by using it as the foundation for your patchwork in this project. For best results, the vest you use should be of a thin, soft, forgiving fabric

*Fig. 3-7. Vest (back) showing detail of patchwork.*

like cotton or corduroy that will be enjoyable to sew through. Use only the vest top fabric; remove any lining or backing.

## MATERIALS

An old vest prepared as described above
Assorted colors of embroidery yarn
Embroidery needle

*Fig. 3-6. Vest (front) showing detail of stitching.*

Assorted fancy fabric scraps: satin,
   velveteen, brocade
Lace or braid trims
3–4 yards fabric binding
Frog closures if desired

## DIRECTIONS

1. Begin covering the vest with fancy fabric
scraps by positioning and pinning a small
irregularly shaped scrap at one edge. Pin a
second scrap along one side of the scrap so
one ragged edge of the first piece is hidden.
With tiny appliqué stitches, turn under the
side of the second scrap where it covers the
first scrap. Do not bother to turn under
edges that run along the outer vest edges.
This will be covered with binding.

2. Proceed in this way to add scraps until
the vest is covered. Be sure all ragged edges
are turned under or covered by other scraps.
Trim any excess fabric from the outer vest
edge.

3. Use decorative embroidery stitching to
embellish the seams where the scrap edges
meet (Fig. 3-8). Add beads, sequins, pearls,
lace, or embroidered motifs. The sample for
this project features antique silks used as
cigarette premiums found at an antiques
shop. Ribbons, buttons, and braids can also
be used for decoration. When adding raised
decorative items, like buttons, to the back,
consider whether they will be uncomfort-

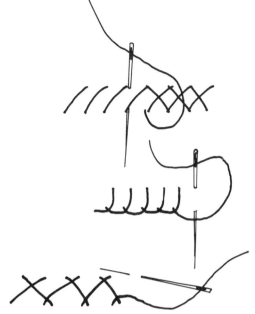

*Fig. 3-8. Crazy quilt stitches. Cross stitch, blanket
stitch, and Herringbone stitch.*

able when leaning against the back of a chair
while wearing your vest.

4. When your embellishing is complete,
bind all the way around the outer edge of
the vest, using a fabric binding to match the
fabrics and colors used in your scraps. Binding a vest is much like binding a quilt, except you will have to mold the binding
around more edges and corners. When all of
the vest edges are bound, add frog or loop-
and-button closures to the front if desired,
or let the front of the vest remain open.

# Chapter Four | Pennsylvania: Amish Quilts

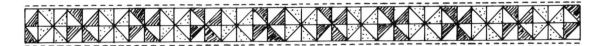

# THE SIMPLE LIFE REFLECTED IN QUILTS

Traveling in and around the hilly green farmlands of Lancaster County, the visitor knows when he or she has arrived in Amish country. The signs of modern life disappear. Suddenly there are no telephone lines or street lights, no television antennae, no satellite dishes. The roads grow narrow. Automobiles are replaced by the occasional horse-drawn buggy (Fig. 4-1).

Visitors to this area are fascinated by

*Fig. 4-1. An Amish horse and buggy are a typical sight on the roads of Lancaster County, Pennsylvania. Photograph courtesy of The People's Place, Intercourse, Pennsylvania.*

their Amish hosts. The Amish adherence to traditional sex roles, lack of anxiety over personal freedom and identity, and disregard for fashion astonish the majority of tourists whose lives are enmeshed in such concerns. Even the casual visitor can sense that what is significant about the Amish way is not the horse-drawn vehicles and plain dress. These are only outward symbols of much more meaningful convictions regarding the importance of worship, the value of community and home life, and a striving for peace and simplicity.

The Amish were attracted to Pennsylvania with its promise of inexpensive farmland and relief from religious persecution as early as the 1690s. Families began immigrating there soon after the Amish separated from the Mennonites. To get a clear picture of this split and what it meant, it is necessary to back up a bit.

The Mennonites were a religious group that had separated from the state church in Switzerland in 1525. Harshly persecuted for their beliefs, they traveled from one European country to another. In time, a portion of Mennonites led by Jacob Ammann (from whom the Amish get their name) formed their own distinct group. Like the Mennonites, they believed in adult baptism and separation of church and state. Unlike the parent group which they had left, they also believed in "shunning" or ostracizing wayward members.[1]

By the middle of the 1700s, many self-sufficient rural Amish farming communities were well established in Pennsylvania. To-day about eighty percent of Amish people live in Pennsylvania, Ohio, and Indiana, but there are Amish in twenty states altogether and in Canada as well.[2]

Currently, Amish needleworkers make quilts using many different printed fabrics and quilt patterns. But that was not always so. Traditional Amish colors, fabrics, and quilt patterns are distinctive. At one time, Amish quilters used only plain solid fabric, dyed by hand using natural dyes. The colors were the same as those employed in sewing homemade Amish clothing. Plenty of black was used, but so were other colors—blues, greens, purples, and dark reds, for instance. These rich tones were used in children's clothing, underdresses, blouses, and in some cases, men's shirts.

Amish color combinations have a refreshing innocence about them. Jonathan Holstein calls this tendency "a unique and gay aggressiveness in color that reflects the Pennsylvania German zest for strong and fundamental living."[3] It has also been suggested that to dress and furnish one's home in the Plain manner makes for a fresh, instinctive use of color—the combining, for instance, of magenta and red in a single quilt.[4] In analyzing traditional Amish quilt color choices, Roberta Horton suggests that orange, yellow and yellow-green were simply avoided.[5]

The way in which Amish quilts differed from other quilts reflected an expression of values. Traditionally, the Amish eschewed patterned fabric, such as calico or chintz, as too fancy or worldly for making

quilts, let alone clothing. Borders were never mitered at the corners. Intricate piecing was considered too time consuming and so was also worldly, as was appliqué which involved the added disgrace of being wasteful of cloth.

Fancy quilting, however, was as decorative as could be. Intricate quilt stitching flourished. It has been speculated that this was because the fancy stitching formed a subdued and unobtrusive pattern.[6] More likely, it reflected an appreciation of function. Quilting holds a quilt together. The more dense the quilting, the less likely the filling is to shift. Beauty in function was appreciated in this work-oriented culture where mere decoration was less esteemed.

Traditionally, three principle Amish quilt patterns were executed far more than any others—Center Diamond, Sunshine and Shadows, and Bars. The design of the Center Diamond pattern is in keeping with traditional values; the large pattern components could be pieced with a minimum of time. To have spent too much time on piecing would have been seen as a needless extravagance. The large fabric expanses of this pattern, with its diamond or large center square set on point, allowed fancy quilt stitching to be seen and appreciated.

Where fabric was probably purchased expressly to make a Center Diamond quilt, with its large fabric expanses, the Sunshine and Shadow pattern made economic use of colorful leftover scraps of cloth. Related in design to the Center Diamond (Fig. 4-2), the Sunshine and Shadow pattern is made

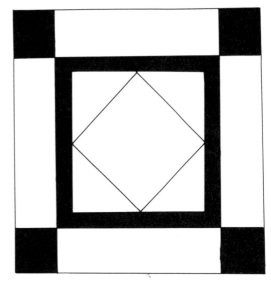

*Fig. 4-2. Center Diamond pattern.*

up of small squares in different colors that radiate out from the center to form the outlines of many diamonds or large squares set on point. Some of the diamond-shaped outlines are of dark fabric, some are of light, suggesting how the pattern got its name. Sometimes a Center Diamond was pieced with a Sunshine and Shadow square in the middle, making an appealing combination.

The small squares of the Sunshine and Shadow pattern are often quilted with straight lines—a cross running through the center of each square. The wide borders allow an expert quilter more of an opportunity to exercise her skills. The pattern and name of the Sunshine and Shadow design still provides an appealing metaphor for the rewards and rigors of the Amish way of life.

The simple Bars pattern has a striking rhymical quality. The stripes are reminiscent of rich, plowed furrows of earth, an image that would have meaning for any Amish farmwoman. Like the Sunshine and Shadows quilt, Bars quilts often feature straight line quilting in the "decorative" center portion of the design and more fancy stitching in the wide borders (Fig. 4-3).

Why did Amish quilts develop as they did? Isolation was a major factor. From the beginning, the Amish maintained their European traditions and remained separate from the rest of American society. Amish women, having little interaction with the outside world, created their own unique quilt patterns and designs.

Amish families that moved to the Midwest were less able to isolate themselves from the American mainstream. Distances were greater than in Pennsylvania. Not always having others of their faith nearby, the Midwest Amish tended to visit and interact more with non-Amish neighbors. Early on, the connection with outsiders or "the English" as non-Amish have been called, resulted in midwestern Amish quilts being made in styles other than the Center Diamond, Sunshine and Shadows, and Bars patterns which were largely used in the original settlement areas.

In recent decades, the self-imposed isolation of the Amish has grown more difficult to maintain. The year 1940 has become a kind of cut-off date for collectors of Amish quilts. Experts recognize that Amish quilts, like Amish culture, have changed and are changing.

Part of that change is the result of tourism. Visitors to Lancaster and nearby areas are eager to visit the Amish which lets them experience another culture without leaving their own country. In a sense, today's tourists have brought a kind of "sunshine and shadow" into Amish life. Ninety percent of Amish quilts made are produced for tourists.[7] In an age in which land becomes more and more scarce, not all Amish families can rely on farming to supply all their needs. The making and selling of quilts provides them with a lucrative pursuit that does not conflict with their values and lifestyle. At the same time, tourists can be intrusive and overly curious. Some, not content with purchasing quilts at shops where Amish goods are sold, do not hesitate to intrude themselves door to door on Amish families.

Quiltmaking has special significance to Amish quilters. Like quilters everywhere, they enjoy their needlework as an outlet for expression and creativity. Moreover, in a world in which television and radio play no part, interactions with friends and neighbors are vital. Sewing, whether at an all-day quilting bee or an impromptu gathering, allows one to remain "useful" while enjoying the company of friends. As is the case anywhere, to give a quilt is to communicate feelings of warmth, protectiveness, and caring. Among the Amish, who somewhat restrain public displays of emotion, quilts also provide a tangible demonstration of love.

Fig. 4-3. Amish Bars Quilt. Photograph courtesy of The People's Place.

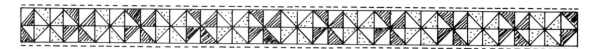

Hard work is a daily feature of life on an Amish farm. Chores are expected to be performed carefully. Yet pride in a job well done is not allowed, as pride is regarded as a sin. But if the Amish way of life is austere, it is not unreasonable. A woman may take pleasure in the work of her hands, regarding her talents as gifts from God and the product of an industrious spirit. Beauty and craftsmanship are greatly valued in Amish culture. So it is that a delicately stitched quilt, a colorful flower garden, or a well-stocked pantry bearing witness to hours of canning, are outlets through which a woman can demonstrate her abilities without shame.

## NOTES

1. Rachel T. Pellman and Joanne Ranck, *Quilts Among the Plain People* (Intercourse, PA: Good Books, 1981), pp. 22–23.

2. Roberta Horton, *An Amish Adventure: A Workbook for Color in Quilts* (Lafayette, CA: C & T Publishing, 1983), p. 3.

3. Jonathan Holstein, *The Pieced Quilt: An Amiercan Tradition* (Boston: Little, Brown, and Co.: 1973), p. 99.

4. Rachel and Kenneth Pellman, *The World of Amish Quilts* (Intercourse, PA: Good Books, 1984), p. 24.

5. Horton, p. 5.

6. Linda Boynton, "Recent Changes in Amish Quilting," *Uncoverings '85*, vol. 6 of the research papers of the American Quilt Study Group, p. 38.

7. Boynton, p. 40.

# TECHNIQUES OF AMISH PATCHWORK

Traditional Amish colors range from rich purples, reds and greens to pale blues, lavenders and pinks. When designing your own color combinations, avoid yellow, orange, and yellow-green for an Amish "feel" to the colors. In planning color schemes for patterns that use large fabric expanses, keep all colors within the same relative intensity. For instance, if using dark purple and teal, add magenta, rather than a pastel pink.

*Plate 1. Peace Quilt (project, Chapter Two) illustrating early American piecing and appliqueing.*

*Plate 2. Early American piecing and appliqueing:
Homespun Hearts Wall Hanging, Pieced Pillow,
and Rose Wreath Pillow (projects, Chapter Two).*

*Plate 7. Tahitian Tifaifai Rose Wall Hanging (project, Chapter Seven). Inset: Tahitian Tifaifai, c. 1940, Rose Bowl Rose featuring ¹/₂" squares. From the collection of Judy Mathieson. Photograph by Jack Mathieson.*

Plate 8. "Tree of Life" Hmong needlework.

Plate 9. (Opposite page) Hmong patchwork. Inset:
Hmong Christmas Star Pillow (project, Chapter
Eight).

*Plate 10. Japanese sashiko wall hangings. (Upper right: project, Chapter 9).*

*Plate 15. "South Hill" quilt illustrating broderie persé technique.*

*Plate 16. Top: Arpilleras. (Right) women tending soup pot (Chilean); (middle) nativity scene (Peruvian); (left) community chores (Chilean). Bottom: Panamanian mola with parrot motif.*

Generally, you will want to avoid most true pastels except in the Sunshine and Shadows pattern where they make an appealing contrast with the richer hues. Remember that colors placed against black appear more intense.

Many traditional Amish quilt tops were pieced on a sewing machine (treadle-style, not electric). But using a modern sewing machine, while not in keeping with Amish values, will not detract from your finished creation. Precise meeting of corners and straight seams in piecing are essential, especially when working with the patterns that utilize large design areas like Center Diamond and Bars.

For best results use all 100% cotton fabrics and be sure to preshrink them. Use black, rather than white quilting thread.

# SUNSHINE AND SHADOWS CRIB QUILT

## Difficulty Level: Challenging

Please review Piecing and Quilting in the chapter on Basic Techniques before beginning. See completed project in color section (Plate 4).

## MATERIALS

1½ yards solid black (from which you will cut small squares and four border strips)
½ yard each of the following: purple, dark lavender, light lavender, mulberry, white, light blue, blue, light pink, and gray
1 yard each of dark pink (from which you will cut small squares, four corner blocks, and 2″ wide binding strips) and slate blue
One 60″ × 60″ square batting
One 60″ × 60″ square backing fabric (black or navy)
Black quilting thread

## DIRECTIONS

1. The following measurements do not include seam allowance. Add the seam allowance before you cut these pieces. Measure and cut out the four black 4″ × 42″ border panels, the four 4″ × 4″ pink corner blocks, and the 2″ wide pink binding. You will need about 4½ yards of binding strips.

2. Trace the small square template onto cardboard. Use it to mark and cut the following squares: 64 black, 24 purple, 24 dark lavender, 24 light lavender, 24 mulberry, 25 white, 28 light blue, 32 blue, 60 slate blue, 40 dark pink, 36 pink, 32 light pink, and 28 gray.

3. Piece separately each row of the center design, beginning with the top row, and using the following as a guide.

Fig. 4-4. Sunshine and Shadows Crib Quilt project.

## TEMPLATE DIAGRAM

*Piecing Diagram*

Black: A; Purple: B; Dark Lavender: C; Light Lavender: D; Mulberry: E; White: F; Light blue: G; Blue: H; Slate Blue: I; Dark Pink: J; Pink: K; Light Pink: L; Gray: M.

Rows 1 and 21: A, B, C, D, E, F, G, H, I, A, J, A, I, H, G, F, E, D, C, B, A.

Rows 2 and 20: B, C, D, E, F, G, H, I, A, J, K, J, A, I, H, G, F, E, D, C, B.

Rows 3 and 19: C, D, E, F, G, H, I, A, J, K, L, M, L, K, J, A, I, H, G, F, E, D, C.

Rows 4 and 18: D, E, F, G, H, I, A, J, K, L, M, L, K, J, A, I, H, G, F, E, D.

Rows 5 and 17: E, F, G, H, I, A, J, K, L, M, I, M, L, J, K, A, I, H, G, F, E.

Rows 6 and 16: F, G, H, I, A, J, K, L, M, I, A, I, M, L, K, J, A, I, H, G, F.

Rows 7 and 15: G, H, I, A, J, K, L, M, A, B, A, I, M, L, K, J, A, I, H, G.

Rows 8 and 14: H, I, A, J, K, L, M, I, A, B, C, B, A, I, M, L, K, J, A, I, H.

Rows 9 and 13: I, A, J, K, L, M, I, A, B, C, D, C, B, A, I, M, L, K, J, A, I.

Rows 10 and 12: A, J, K, L, M, I, A, B, C, D, E, D, C, B, A, I, M, L, K, J, A.

Row 11: J, K, L, M, I, A, B, C, D, E, F, E, D, C, B, A, I, M, L, K, J.

4. Join the rows, matching seams carefully as you go, to complete the center design.

*Templates for this project look like this and are found at the back of the book.*

5. Join the pink corners and the black borders to the center design to complete the pieced top.

6. Place the backing fabric right side down on a clean floor or large work surface and tape it in place so it will not shift. Place over this the batting and the quilt top right side up. Pin and baste the three layers together.

7. Quilt the project using diagonal lines of quilting. The quilting lines will run through the corners of each small square, forming a cross in the center of each square.

8. Quilt the borders using the wave pattern template and marking the design on the fabric with a chalk wheel. The pink corner squares of the sample project are quilted with a cross-hatched circle design. You may want to try a similar design, using the sample project as a guide, or substitute with a quilted heart in each corner, using the heart-shaped quilting template provided for the Homespun Hearts Wall Hanging project.

9. Bind the quilt, using the pink binding strips to complete the project.

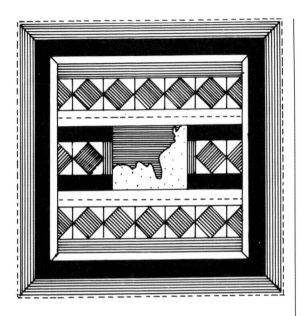

# Chapter Five

# Florida: Seminole Patchwork

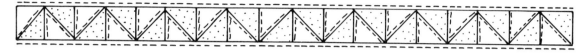

# NATIVE TRADITION CONTINUES IN FLORIDA

For those of us who are used to the changing seasons, southern Florida appears tropical indeed. Away from the cities, palm trees and towering southern pines grow wild by the roadside. Trees of all kinds are festooned with hanging Spanish moss and creeping vines.

Dense Florida swamplands, like the Everglades, are home to a wide variety of exotic plant and animal life: the mangrove with its tangle of thick roots; prickly-looking little epiphytes or air plants; and flowering cactus. Birdwatchers who visit can still see shy roseate spoonbills, wood storks, and delicate white egrets. Newcomers always remark on the anhinga or snake-bird, an eerie link between reptiles and birds, that looks like a snake as it swims the water hunting fish, but is more often seen standing in brush, drying its wings which it must do before it can fly.

The swamplands encompass submerged wetlands, as well as large areas of pine woods, open grassy glades, raised islands of jungle growth called hammocks. The different tribes of Native Americans who lived here planted their crops in the rich soil of these elevated areas.

The Florida swamplands can be threatening, inhabited by alligators, rattlesnakes and the rare, deadly coral snake. It was into this beautiful, dangerous environment that the people we now call the Seminole retreated during the 18th century.

There were Indian tribes in Florida long before the Seminole arrived—Timucua, Calusa, Tekesta, Apalachee. Because of contact with European diseases, the majority were wiped out. By the time the Seminole came along, the region was largely uninhabited.[1]

The Seminole originally belonged to the Creek confederation of tribes. They lived in what is now Alabama and Georgia, and migrated to northern Florida in the early 1700s when it was still claimed by the Spanish. (The name Seminole may have roots in the spanish word *cimaron* or "wild," although it has also been defined as "runaway" and "pioneer.") By 1774, Florida had come under British rule and Naturalist William Bartram described a "Seminole" village which he happened upon in his travels. He observed boys fishing with "rods and lines," women "hoeing corn," a "carefully pruned" orange grove, and "several hundred acres of cleared land." "Thus," he concluded, "they enjoy a superabundance of the necessaries and conveniences of life, with the security of person and property, the two great concerns of mankind. . . No cruel enemy to dread, nothing to give them disquietude, but the gradual encroachments of the white people."[2]

Bartram's words were to prove all too prophetic. By the early 1800s, Seminole villages harbored numbers of black slaves who had escaped from their masters, as well as renegade whites. In 1818, the U.S. government responded to the objections of slave owners and sent troops to Florida. The first Seminole War ended in defeat for the Indians. Soon after, the United States government purchased Florida from Spain, which had reclaimed the area. Indians there were urged to sell their lands and move west to reservations. Many did so, but others fled farther south and into the Florida swamps where they vowed to stay.

The result was the Second Seminole War. Chief Osceola led the Native Indian resistance until he was tricked into discussing peace terms under a flag of truce. He died in prison a few months later.

In time, the majority of Indians moved west to the reservations. A small group, however, retreated deep into the Everglades where they lived for decades in virtual isolation.

Many men had been killed during the years of fighting. As a result, women came to dominate the family structure more than ever before. Even today, the Seminole are a matriarchal society. Modern Seminole women are regarded as heads of families. They own the property and their decisions in domestic matters are final. The men, however, make the decisions regarding tribal affairs in which women have little say.[3]

When the Seminole first arrived in Florida, they had worn traditional buckskin clothing. This proved too warm for southern Florida's hot, often humid climate, although mosquitos and other insects made protective clothing a must. From traders, the Indians obtained fabrics which were made into blouses and long, full skirts for women, and smock-like shirts for men which were worn with buckskin leggings.

By the 1880s, the Seminoles were routinely wearing clothes made of calico, gingham, cotton, and flannel. Early photographs show men wearing knee-length tunics decorated with colorful braids and solid-color strips of cloth. Women wore ankle-length skirts with similar decoration and soft, light-colored capes.

Around the turn of the century, traders began supplying sewing machines to Seminole women. With the arrival of this popular appliance, the braid and solid fabric strip decorations began to be replaced by more intricately patterned fabric strips. These colorful geometric bands were assembled and inserted into the garments. For perhaps the first time since the creation of the needle, the invention of a tool resulted in a new form of patchwork. The technique of Seminole piecing was born.

Today, the Immokalee Seminole Indian Reservation in Immokalee, Florida is one of a number of reservations where the Florida Seminole live today. Bordering the reservation are rows of small white concrete houses. The first floor of one of these has been given over as the temporary headquarters for the Native Arts and Crafts Center.

The original center burned down and is being rebuilt. In the meantime, five Seminole women ranging in age from about 20 to 60 are seated at recently donated sewing machines making clothing decorated with Seminole patchwork. The clothing will be sold at the Center.

These women are not dressed in the ankle-length patchwork skirts and traditional capes of their forebears. They do not wear the bead necklaces which, in earlier times, were piled high on a woman's neck up to her chin. A couple of them wear blue jeans; the others, the same kind of mid-calf-length patchwork skirts on which they now work. The sound of the songs on the radio blends musically with their occasional sentences to each other spoken in native language.

The room in which the women work is cheerful, bright, and filled with natural light from the large windows. The airiness of the work room is perhaps unconsciously imitative of the *chickee*, the traditional Seminole home—an elevated platform with a palmetto thatched roof, open on all sides with simple log roof supports.

Some of the women sew clothing. The others work on colorful patchwork strips used to decorate a variety of clothes including skirts and blouses for women; shirts, vests and jackets for men; pinafores for

*Fig. 5-1. Needleworkers at the Seminole Indian Reservation in Immokolee, Florida use sewing machines to produce their intricate designs.*

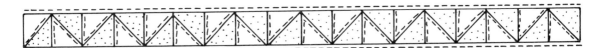

girls. Each color in the intricate patchwork is a separate fabric. The sewing of a single strip could take weeks if done by hand. On a sewing machine, with practice, it takes a matter of hours (Fig. 5-1). Black-haired Indian dolls with heads made of palmetto leaves and dressed in the fancy patchwork are also crafted here (Fig. 5-2).

The Indian needlewomen construct their patchwork by horizontally joining long strips of solid, brightly colored cotton fabric. The strips have been torn evenly by hand, rather than cut. After the strips are sewn together horizontally, they are cut more or less vertically and the new, vertical strips are resewn. The variety of patterns made by creative positioning of the vertical strips is astonishing. If the strips are simply turned on the diagonal and joined, an intriguing network of triangles and squares emerges. Different ways of positioning the strips can

*Fig. 5-2. Even dolls made of palmetto leaves are dressed in colorful Seminole pieced clothing.*

yield fresh patterns. Some of the patterns are traditional, but new ones are always being invented. In this way, the Seminole needleworkers keep their relatively young craft tradition alive and vibrant for future generations to enjoy.

## NOTES

1. Merwyn S. Garbarino, *Big Cypress: a Changing Seminole Community* (New York: Holt, Rinehart and Winston, 1972), p. 9.

2. William Bartram, *The Travels of William Bartram, Naturalist's Edition* (New Haven: Yale University Press, 1958), pp. 59–60, pp. 118–119.

3. Margaret Brandebourg, *Seminole Patchwork* (New York: Sterling Publishing Company, 1987), p. 10.

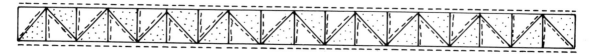

# TECHNIQUES OF SEMINOLE PATCHWORK

Although a finished article of Seminole patchwork features many tiny fabric shapes, the actual construction involves the handling, not of little pieces of fabric, but of long strips. This makes it easier to do than it appears at first. The technique eliminates the need for templates and the colorful strips can be made up surprisingly quickly. It must, however, be done on a sewing machine. Only machine stitching is strong enough to allow the strips to be cut apart without causing them to disintegrate.

In creating your own Seminole-style patchwork, choose bright solid cottons for the design. Patterned fabrics will muddy the design and should be avoided. Colors may be set against black for striking effects. Solid colors that provide good contrast when placed against one another will bring out the intricacy of the design. If the colors tend to melt into each other, the geometric effect will be less powerful. Try colors that are set well apart from each other on the color wheel like turquoise, yellow, and red, for instance, instead of blue, turquoise and green.

If you are going to follow the traditional method of tearing, rather than cutting fabric strips, you will want to test your fabric beforehand. Be sure that it tears evenly and accurately along the straight weave of the fabric. Otherwise, you will want to use a rotary cutter for producing fast and even fabric strips. Try to choose fabrics of similar weight. Puckering can occur when fabrics of different weights are sewn together. Choose a neutral thread color for sewing. A $\frac{1}{4}''$ seam allowance is sufficient for joining strips together securely so that they will not fray even if washed.

To save time in sewing pairs of small patchwork strips together, chain-sew the pairs. That is, do not take up the presser foot and cut the thread between the pairs.

*Fig. 5-3. Front of coat showing Seminole patchwork.*

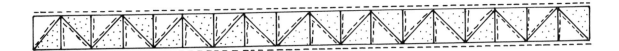

*Fig. 5-4. Back of coat.*

Pull the sewn pair to the back, leaving an inch or so of uncut thread and begin sewing the next pair together. Do the same for the next pair. This means the pairs will be connected by thread. When you are ready to work with the pairs, cut apart the "chain" and sew them as called for by your pattern.

*Fig. 5-5. Skirt showing Seminole patchwork.*

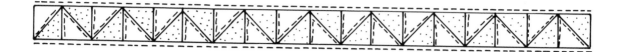

# BAND AND APRON

Difficulty Level:
Easy to Moderate

Please review Machine Piecing in the chapter on Basic Techniques before beginning. See completed project in color section (Plate 5).

The colorful patchwork band described in this project is designed to decorate an apron, but you can make your band of greater or lesser length and use it to embellish a skirt hem or other article of clothing. The project calls for solid color fabrics, preferably pre-shrunk 100% cotton.

To obtain the needed fabric strips, tear the fabric from selvage edge to selvage edge or use a rotary cutter.

This band design is a simple one. By changing the width of the strips or varying the number of strips used, you can create a variety of different patterns. The design possibilities for Seminole pieced work in general, however, are endless and some patterns are quite complex. As you experiment with different combinations, you will discover many more designs.

*Fig. 5-6. Detail of Band and Apron project.*

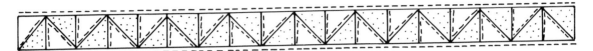

## MATERIALS

1 yard black (apron skirt)
Two 2½" × 36" long strips black (apron ties)
Six 3" wide × 45" long strips blue
Three 1½" wide × 45" long strips turquoise
Three 1½" wide × 45" long strips red
Three 1½" wide × 45" long strips purple
Black sewing thread
Clear plastic ruler with grid markings

## DIRECTIONS

*The Patchwork Band*

1. Iron the strips. Along one long edge, sew one turquoise strip to one red strip using a ¼" seam allowance. Do the same for the remaining turquoise and red strips.

2. Sew one purple strip to one turquoise/red strip as above. Do the same with the remaining strips.

3. Use the rule to mark each strip in 1½" increments. Draw a line across the width of the strip at each 1½" mark. Cut each strip widthwise along the lines you have marked. This will give you cut-apart strip widths of three colors—a "triad."

4. Decide how you want to join the triads. They can be joined (pattern A) straight up and down giving a sort of checkerboard effect at top and bottom and a red line in the middle. Or, (pattern B) turned slightly on the diagonal, they create a pattern of squares and rectangles.

5. Sew the "triads" in pairs, depending on the pattern you have chosen. Then join the pairs. Continue until all of the sections are joined to complete the strip.

6. If you have chosen pattern A, go on to the next step. If you have chosen pattern B, place your ruler over the outer margin of the top of the pieced band. Allowing for a ¼" seam allowance from the tip of each center square, draw a line across the top of the band. Cut the excess fabric along this line to make the band top even. You will be cutting off the triangle points along the top. Do the same for the bottom of the band.

*The Apron*

1. Sew the black strips for the apron ties together along one short edge to make a tie/waistband 72" long. Fold down the middle to make it half as wide and iron the fold.

2. Measure your waist front from right to left to determine how wide you want the apron skirt. Center this measurement in the exact middle of the tie/waistband and mark. (Find the center by folding the tie/waistband in half.)

3. With right sides together, sew the folded tie/waistband along the short right end,

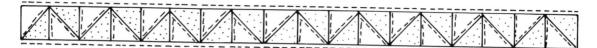

down the long side up to the first waistband mark. Use a ¼″ seam allowance. Do the same for the other side. The waistband section of the tie/waistband is left unsewn.

4. Turn the tie/waistband right side out. Notice that along the waistband section of the tie/waistband, there is excess seam allowance. Turn this under on each side and iron.

5. Place the yard of black fabric (black fabric rectangle) on your work surface lengthwise so that the short sides are to the left and right. Measure from your waist to where you want the hem of your apron to fall. The length from top to bottom of the black fabric rectangle should be about the length you want your apron to be from waistband to hem. Trim away the extra, maintaining an even rectangle.

6. On one short side, turn under the edge of the black fabric rectangle once and then once again to hide the ragged edge. Pin and sew on a machine or use a hem stitch if

sewing by hand. Do the same for one long side and the remaining short side to form the apron skirt.

7. Working from the top of the apron skirt (the remaining long ragged edge), gather the skirt in small pleats and pin to the waistband. Hide the ragged apron skirt edge under the folded edge of the waistband. Pin and top sew the waistband to the apron skirt.

8. All along the lower part of the skirt, measure 3″ up from the bottom. Mark this and cut off a 3″ strip from the bottom of the apron skirt. Set aside for a bottom border.

9. Join the patchwork band to the main part of the apron along the new bottom edge. Turn under and sew the ragged side edges of the patchwork band.

10. Sew the black 3″ bottom border to the rest of the apron along the remaining long patchwork band edge to complete the project.

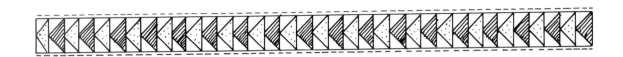

# Part Two: SOUTH SEAS ISLANDS

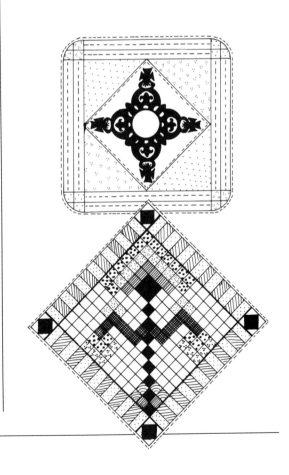

# Chapter Six

# Hawaii: Snowflake Quilting

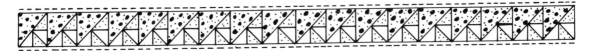

# EARLY MISSIONARY INFLUENCE

Like a beautiful necklace, the Hawaiian islands lie strewn upon the Pacific. Formed by ancient volcanoes built up from the ocean floor, Hawaii is a collection of rock and coral islets, sandy atolls, and eight main islands: Hawaii, Maui, Kahoolawe, Molokai, Lanai, Oahu, Kauai, and Niihau. Much of Hawaii, known as Owhyhee to early western explorers and sailors, offers a breathtaking landscape of rugged mountains, active volcanoes, white beaches and green jungle. The lushness of the remaining Hawaiian rain forest makes it easy to see why early Hawaiian-style quilters naturally turned for their motifs to the bountiful trees, fruits and flowers that surrounded them.

Although Spanish, Dutch, and Japanese explorers may have stopped here as early as the 1500s, most of the world did not know of these islands until 1778 when Captain Cook of the British Navy reached them. He called them the Sandwich Islands for the Earl of Sandwich, the first lord of the British Admiralty. Following this, other explorers and traders began to arrive. The islands became a major stopping point on the Pacific trade route and, early on, fabric was a welcome import.

The islanders did not have a native woven cloth. Their environment produces no fibers truly suitable for spinning like cotton, linen, wool, or silk, which, when woven, made a stable cloth. Instead, their clothes and bed linens were traditionally made of tapa cloth, the pounded and dyed bark of the mulberry plant.

An early account of tapa cloth pointed out: "this cloth, from its texture, is, when wetted, extremely apt to get damaged, in which state it tears like moist paper; great care, therefore, is always taken to keep it dry, or to have it carefully dried when it is wetted."[1]

The islanders spent much of their time in water-related activities. Once trading ships began to arrive on a regular basis, cloth was eagerly sought after. Hawaiians quickly developed a taste as well for European and American-style clothing. As early as 1817, some Hawaiian women were recorded as wearing robe-like calico dresses.[2]

Small wonder there was so much interest shown by four high-ranking Hawaiian women in the sewing skills of the first group of missionary women to visit the islands. The ship *Thaddeus* arrived on March 30, 1820, after a five-month voyage from Boston. It carried the first American missionaries and their wives to the islands. Four royal Hawaiian ladies visited the wives of several missionaries on board. They were eager for their foreign guests to design and make a dress in the latest American style for one of the women. The seven missionary wives, primly dressed in close-fitting, long-

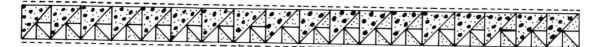

skirted dresses and no doubt scandalized by scant native clothing, were happy to comply.

Lucy Thurston, one of the women on board the *Thaddeus* wrote: "Monday morning, April 3rd, the first sewing circle was formed that the sun ever looked down upon in this Hawaiian realm. Kalakua, queen dowager, was directress. She requested all the seven white ladies to take seats with them on mats. . . Mrs. Holman and Mrs. Ruggles were executive officers, to ply scissors and prepare the work. . . The four native women of distinction were furnished with calico patchwork to sew—a new employment to them."[3]

Sewing, not just of patchwork, but of any kind was new to these high-ranking Hawaiian ladies who would not have been expected to do work of any sort in their own culture. The response of missionary wives in giving their visitors bits of patchwork to sew was a logical one. They may well have assumed their guests were eager to learn to sew dresses on their own, and sewing simple patches was how the missionary wives had learned to sew themselves as children.

Hawaiian quilting as we know it, however, did not really begin on board the *Thaddeus*. Giving sewing lessons became a regular part of the missionary wives' activities as did teaching in the missionary schools that were gradually established. Much of the sewing that was done, however, was geared toward clothing. Missionaries encouraged the islanders to dress in more "Western" style and often gave them the means to do so by teaching sewing and providing cloth.

In 1843, in her letter to a friend in Illinois, Fidelia Coan describes teaching her students the art of quilting to make outerwear: "I have found it a very pleasant reward to be able to give the girls a bit of fitted patchwork, each as large as the sheet upon which (sic) I am writing. Of these pieces they will each eventually make a small quilt. Something like a Spanish poncho to wear in cool or rainy weather."[4]

Having been taught basic sewing skills, native Hawaiians proceeded to create an indigenous style of quiltmaking that is truly breathtaking. Hawaiian quilts, with their "paper snowflake" method of construction, are very different from traditional American patchwork quilts. They feature a single, large lace-like motif or a motif and border cut from one piece of fabric (Fig. 6-1). The design is appliquéd to a background fabric and the contrasting ground peeks through cut-out "windows" within the lacy appliqué. Freehand lines of quilting surround the design in a technique known as echo quilting, although early quilts were more often quilted in an all-over pattern of straight lines or diamonds.

It is not known exactly when Hawaiian quilts in their unique "paper snowflake" style were first made. It has been suggested that the early missionary wives may have taught their students the craft of fancy paper-cutting, a popular Victorian pastime leading, in the hands of native Hawaiians, to this distinctive quilting style. What

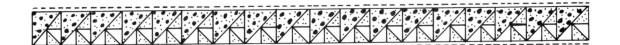

*Fig. 6-1. Ka Ua Kani Lehua (The Rain that Rustles Lehua Blossoms), artist unknown, Island of Hawaii, c.1900. Photograph courtesy of Honolulu Academy of Arts.*

*Fig. 6-2. Na Kalaunu Me Na Kahili (Crowns and Kahilis), by Mrs. William Harrison Rice, c.1886. Photograph courtesy of Honolulu Academy of Arts.*

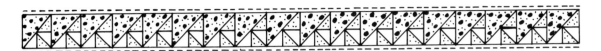

seems most likely to some researchers, however, is that the technique of creating a design from folded and cut fabric was introduced to the islanders in the 1860s by Pennsylvania Dutch missionaries. This ethnic group was known for snowflake-style quilts as well as the craft of scissors cuttings known as Scherenschnitte which may have been related to its appliqué tradition.

An additional influence on the snowflake patterns of Hawaiian quilts was the traditional motifs used to decorate tapa cloth. Often these cloth designs were lacelike and repetitive, like delicate folded inkblots. Like the quilt designs which they probably influenced, they suggest a graceful, exotic habitat.

American pioneer women enjoyed a host of quilt-related quilting superstitions and symbols. (Hearts on a wedding quilt brought bad luck, for instance, and a young girl who slept under a new quilt would dream of her future husband.) Hawaiian quiltmakers took this tradition one step further and enshrouded the creation of their quilts in mystery and symbolism (Fig. 6-2). Even today, each quilter's design is regarded as uniquely personal. An individual quilt is felt to be uniquely imbued with the spirit of its maker.[5]

## NOTES

1. Archibald Campbell, *A Voyage Round the World from 1806–1812* (reprint, Honolulu: University Press of Hawaii, 1979), p. 203.

2. V.M. Golounin, *Around the World on the Kamchatka 1817–1819* (Honolulu: The University Press of Hawaii, 1977), p. 178.

3. Sally Garoutte, "Uses of Textiles in Hawaii: 1820–1850," *Uncoverings 1985*, p. 149.

4. Garoutte, p. 155.

5. Elizabeth Akana, *The Quilt Digest* (San Francisco: Kirakofe and Kile: 1984), p. 75.

# TECHNIQUES OF HAWAIIAN QUILTING

Hawaiian-style quilts are done in appliqué technique. A single large piece of fabric is used for the applied part of the design. The motif, cut from this, is sewn down onto a contrasting background fabric (often white). The contrast between motif and back-

ground, as well as the use of solid colors rather than prints, make for a bold, graphic image. Some traditional Hawaiian quilts feature a white appliqué on a colored background, but this is more difficult to do well. The seam allowance is more likely to show under the edge of a white appliqué on a colored background, distracting attention away from a strong design.

Folding the fabric motif just like a child's paper snowflake ensures geometric perfection. The top fabric is folded in layers and the motif cut like a scissors cutting. Folding also enables the quilter to position the snowflake precisely in the center of the background fabric. Both motif and background are folded in eighths and the folds ironed (Fig. 6-3). When both are opened out again, the center is clearly delineated by the ironed fold lines which allow for perfect positioning all the way out to the corners. The motif is then pinned and basted to the background. Only after basting is the motif appliquéd in place. Repeated "waves" of echo quilting both within the motif and around the outside of it serve to highlight and redefine the basic pattern.

In sewing your own Hawaiian-style quilt, be sure to choose colors with high contrast. One pastel on another, for instance, may yield disappointing results. Motif fabrics traditionally are rich, brilliant colors—mustard, royal blue, red, or grass green.

For projects under 44″ to 45″ square, you will have little trouble cutting a single appliqué in "paper snowflake" style. In doing large projects, you may want to use brightly colored sheets for both appliqué and background fabric to avoid working

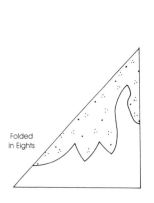

Folded in Eights

Fig. 6-3. Oak Leaf and Acorn pattern showing folding technique.

with seams. Otherwise, before you begin cutting, sew the appliqué fabric widths together lengthwise with the seam falling where the middle of the appliqué will be. Use same color thread and press the seams open.

The makers of early Hawaiian quilts were inspired by their tropical environment and the things of beauty they found there. Their patterns suggest intricate corals, lush foliage, and delicate flowers. You can use the pattern provided for this project. You can also look at pictures of traditional quilts to get ideas for your own, more personal design. Or, like the native Hawaiians, you can go outdoors to your own environment and choose a motif that pleases you from the leaves, branches, fruits, and flowers that your eye discovers.

Experiment by cutting a variety of snowflakes in paper. Fold a square of paper in half three times to make eight divisions in the square when it is unfolded. The middle of the appliqué is the point where the greatest number of folds come together. Work with this point down so as to keep in mind where the middle of your design will fall when the cutout is opened out.

Try cutting some circular snowflake designs and some square ones. Try making some with a border (as in the project) and others without. Be sure your pattern will allow for a $1/4''$ seam allowance to be added all the way around for turning under. Traditionally, this seam allowance is a scant $1/8''$, and you can choose to make it so, but if your appliqué experience is limited, you may find $1/4''$ seam allowances challenging enough.

You can substitute your own design for the one in the project by checking first to be sure the measurements are roughly the same. If you need to correct the size of a motif, do it on a photocopy machine that has enlargement/reduction capability. Put a piece of black paper behind the cut-and-folded acute triangle.

After you have transferred your motif to fabric, you will cut it out, adding seam allowance as you cut. When finished, open it out. At this point any inward-turning curves need to be clipped. When first laid out on the background fabric, your motif will not much resemble your original design because it will include added seam allowance all the way around.

The motif should be basted to the background using fairly large stitches in a contrasting color so they can easily be pulled out later. Basting stitches should be about $1/2''$ in from the raw fabric edge. Be sure the appliqué is basted closely to the background so it will not shift, since shifting causes puckering.

Start from the center of the appliqué and work out, using matching thread to turn under and sew the appliqué to the background fabric. Turn the raw edge of the appliqué under a little at a time, rolling it under with the needle as you sew. Use an overcast or blind stitch to hold the turned under edges in place and take fairly close stitches.

Quilting is traditionally done in the

same color as the background fabric. The lines of quilting are usually judged by eye without being marked on the fabric. The quilting follows the outline of the appliqué design in waves about ½" apart. Where two lines of quilt stitches come together, they can converge to a single line of quilting.

To begin quilting, start in the center (as for any quilt) and run lines of quilting inside the appliqué to follow the outline of the motif. Then on the outside of the motif, run additional, similar quilting lines to follow the motif's outline. Continue to add additional "outlines" to the outer edges of the quilt.

Traditionally, Hawaiian quilts are bound off in one of two ways. The backing edge and top edge can both be turned in and then sewn together with a whip stitch. Or, a thin binding that matches the appliqué fabric may be added.

# APPLE TREE WALL QUILT    Difficulty Level: Moderate

Please review Appliqué and Quilting in the chapter on Basic Techniques before beginning.

The central motif in this project was inspired by a natural motif in the author's New England environment—an ancient, twisted apple tree. The solid appliqué fabric is in the shade known as "apple-green."

## MATERIALS

24" × 24" square of green solid
Four 2" × 30" strips of green solid for binding
24" × 24" square of muslin background fabric (with corners slightly rounded or "softened")
30" × 30" square of batting (with corners rounded)
30" × 30" square of muslin backing fabric (with corners rounded)

Sewing thread to match solid green fabric
Off-white quilting thread

## DIRECTIONS

1. Fold the green fabric square three times to get a triangle. Trace the snowflake-style template and transfer the design to the fabric triangle. Only the turning under line for the fabric is marked. You will need to add a ¼" seam allowance all the way around the design as you cut out the fabric.

2. Cut out the marked appliqué pattern (Fig. 6-5). It is in two pieces—a center motif and a border. Be sure to add a ¼" seam allowance to all edges as you cut.

3. Clip all concave curves slightly to aid in turning the edges under as you sew. Fold the muslin background fabric in eighths and

*Fig. 6-4. Apple Tree Wall Quilt project.*

iron. Do the same for the border and center motif.

4. Position the border and the center motif on the background fabric. Use the ironed lines as a guide in lining the design correctly on the background. Pin all in place, using straight pins, then baste the design down fairly tightly to avoid having the appliqué shift as you sew.

5. Sew the appliqué in place, turning under the raw edge of the appliqué as you sew. Sew the center appliqué first and then the border. (Don't turn under the outer border edge that is even with the backing fabric edges.)

6. Tape the 30″ × 30″ muslin backing fabric flat on a table surface or clean floor. Position the batting on top, then the appliquéd

## TEMPLATE DIAGRAM

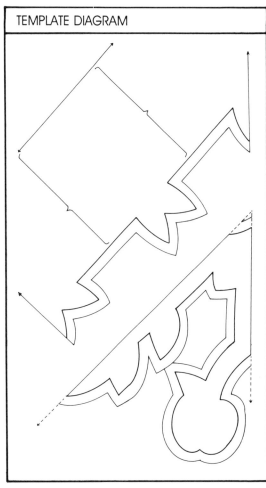

*Templates for this project look like this and are found at the back of the book.*

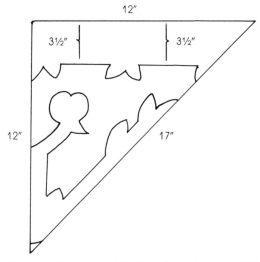

*Fig. 6-5. Proper positioning of templates on folded cloth.*

top fabric. Pin, then baste all three layers in place.

7. Remove the tape and any pins. Quilt the basted project from the center out, using "echo quilting" or lines of quilting ½" apart in waves that follow the design of the appliqué. Use your eye to guide you, rather than marking the lines of quilting on the fabric.

8. Bind the project with a thin ½" binding using the four 2" × 30" strips of green fabric. Add a sleeve for hanging to the back if desired.

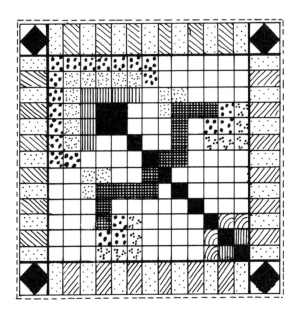

# Chapter Seven

# Tahiti: Tifaifai

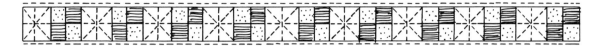

# PATCHWORK FROM PARADISE

Traveling southeast from Hawaii, the visitor arrives at the island of Tahiti, one of the Society Islands of the South Pacific. Here is where artist Paul Gauguin lived and painted for years, "fascinated by golden figures in streams or on the sea-shore."[1] Here is Henri Matisse's "isle of thoughtless indolence and pleasure"[2] where he collected inspiring memories of light and form. They were memories upon which he would draw years later when elderly, ill, and in need, perhaps, of thoughts of warmth and light. His recollections helped him to create an intriguing new art form, his paper cutouts, which inspire so many quilters.

Abundant with rushing torrents of fresh water, flowers, fruits, color and sunlight, little hourglass-shaped Tahiti is surrounded by a protective coral reef. The people have always lived on the flat, fertile strip of land that runs along the coast. The interior of the island, made up of steep verdant mountains is, even today, largely uninhabited.

The underwater world of the island is every bit as striking as that on land. Here one finds bright coral in colors of the rainbow—yellow, pink, and blue—and fish as colorful as the coral amid which they swim. It is a fierce tidal realm inhabited by hungry crabs, stinging anemones, and tenacious clams which, once clamped upon their prey, seldom let go.

Patchwork came to Tahiti, as it did to most of the South Pacific, through the efforts of European and American missionaries. Patchwork bedcoverings in this part of the world are known as tifaifai. They are not quilts in the strict sense as they have no middle batting layer and are not quilted. They are dazzling needlework pictures, often done in a shimmery mosaic style of hundreds of tiny colorful squares.

Tahitians, like Hawaiians and other Polynesian peoples, traditionally had no woven cloth. Here too, tapa was pounded and painted or printed with natural dyes.

On March 5, 1797, the HMS *Duff*, missionary ship from Great Britain, landed off the coast of Tahiti. The island had first become known to the western world as the result of a British exploration team under Samuel Wallis that had arrived in 1767. Thirty years later, eighteen missionaries, six

*Fig. 7-1. Rarotongan women work together on a piecework Tifaifai. Photograph by Joyce Hammond.*

women among them, settled in Tahiti and it was these women who introduced quilting to the islanders. We can only speculate as to the missionary wives' disappointment that their needle skills were adopted so much more readily by these ingenuous natives than was their religion.

That Tahitians rapidly came to appreciate woven cloth is evidenced by the fact that they were growing newly introduced cotton plants as early as 1820 (the same year in which American missionaries first arrived in Hawaii). All had not gone smoothly for the missionaries in the intervening years, however. Tribal wars had flared and many of the new arrivals had fled. In time, however, things became more peaceful. King Pomare II converted to Christianity, as did many of his followers. More missionaries arrived and quilting was spread both by them and by native travelers between the island groups—the Cook Islands, Austral Islands and others. Over the years, different islands developed distinctive regional styles depending on the sewing techniques that had been encouraged in a particular area and the islanders' ingenuity in translating the new skills into something uniquely their own.

Today, Tahiti is a French overseas territory. One year after British explorer Samuel Wallis claimed the island for England, French navigator Louis Antoine de Bougainville claimed it for France. The island became a French protectorate in 1842.

Today, the traditional art form of tifaifai remains strong in Tahiti. Large unquilted patchwork tifaifai coverlets are often given as a gift to someone in the community to express love, respect, or sympathy. The person receiving the tifaifai is ceremonially wrapped in it, a visual expression of a protective community "enveloping" its special ones.

As with the makers of Hawaiian quilts, the creators of tifaifai are protective of the originality of their designs. Sharing designs is uncommon and the feeling of protective secrecy regarding patterns adds to their mystique.

As a result of inter-island travel and resettlement, a variety of tifaifai styles are practiced by women in Tahiti. Both appliquéing and piecing techniques are used. Some designs are closest in spirit to Hawaiian style patterns, others resemble traditional western overall pieced patterns (as opposed to block patterns), and still others are distinctively Polynesian in flavor.

Appliqué tifaifai or tifaifai pa'oti are similar to Hawaiian style designs. Unlike Hawaiian quilts, which are true quilts, the tifaifai pa'oti are made with two layers of fabric and are not quilted. In addition, where the Hawaiian pattern design is traditionally folded in eighths before being cut, the tifaifai version is folded in fourths.[3] Solid colors are usually used. Traditional colors are red on white or white on green, but today, many color combinations are used. Most women, however, continue to favor natural colors such as green for a leafy breadfruit design (Figs. 7-2 and 7-3).

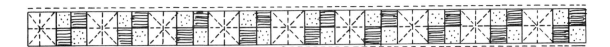

*Fig. 7-2. Hawaiian Breadfruit pattern.*

---

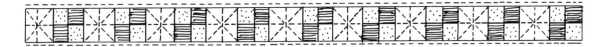

*Fig. 7-3. Tahitian Breadfruit pattern.*

In addition, Tahitians produce free-style appliqué designs as well as a floral style of design that originated on nearby Rarotonga, one of the Cook Islands. Free-style designs often portray colorful images from Tahitian life (people, trees, fruits or flowers) in an informal arrangement. The Rarotongan floral style uses large floral appliqués in many different colors usually organized in a loosely symmetrical decorative manner.

Among the pieced traditions is tifaifai pu, an overall patchwork design made up of tiny geometric shapes, often squares, each as little as 1″ wide. Some tifaifai pu are reminiscent of our traditional pieced patterns Trip Around the World, or Sunshine and Shadows.

Traditionally, much of the work done by women on Tahiti was done communally. Making patchwork tops fitted easily into familiar group work habits. Even today, much of Tahitian patchwork is made as a group. The large overall pattern of a tifaifai pu, for example, is broken down, usually into eight triangular sections. The tiny scraps that make up a section are strung on a string in a specific sewing order and handed out to different women to sew together. Later, the finished sections are joined.[4]

Expanding on the same design concept of many tiny joined squares is the pieced mosaic, perhaps the most inventive style of tifaifai pu and characteristically Polynesian. Little squares, 1″ across or less, are pieced together to form complicated pictures or images. Many pieced mosaic designs depict flowers in brilliant varied hues, suggesting a three-dimensional play of light and shadow on colored petals. The painterly fashion in which the colors are set against one another makes this style of patchwork especially challenging to design, coordinate, and sew.

Though widely practiced in Tahiti, the mosaic style is not indigenous. On the island of Rurutu, one of the Austral Islands, mosaic style patchwork is known as iripiti; and on Rarotonga of the Cook Islands it is called tivaevae taorei. Exactly how and when it arrived in Tahiti is not known, but today this style is highly valued and produced by many accomplished Tahitian needleworkers.

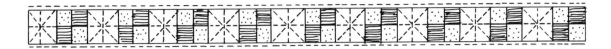

## NOTES

1. Bengt Danielsson, *Gauguin in the South Seas* (New York: Doubleday, 1966), p. 96.

2. John Elderfield, *The Cut-Outs of Henri Matisse* (New York: George Braziller, 1978), p. 32.

3. Joyce D. Hammond, *Tifaifai and Quilts of Polynesia* (Honolulu: University of Hawaii Press, 1986), p. 2.

4. Vicki Poggioli, *Patterns from Paradise: The Art of Tahitian Quilting* (Pittstown, NJ: Mainstreet Press, 1988), p. 32.

# TECHNIQUES OF TIFAIFAI

As previously discussed, there are different styles of tifaifai. For now, we will concentrate on the mosaic style of tifaifai pu. Good, sturdy 100% cotton solids are best for this, as for most patchwork styles. To ensure durability of your finished creation, be sure to preshrink fabric and take care not to mix 100% cottons with polyester/cotton blends. Using mixed fabrics in the top or one kind for the top and another for the backing can cause the fabrics in finished tifaifai to wear and pull differently, creating distortion in the pattern and loosening stitches.

If you have never invested in a rotary cutter and self-healing cutting mat, now may be the time to do so. You can, of course, choose instead to cut fabric into strips with scissors and hand cut the strips into the tiny squares that make up the design, but it is more time-consuming than making a few swipes with the cutting wheel. Besides, using a rotary cutter is fun.

A rotary cutter can cut through several layers of fabric at once. This will not be a consideration for making the project offered here. But if, having tried the project, you decide to go on and make a large mosaic tifaifai of your own design, it may be helpful in cutting out the hundreds of tiny pieces that will be needed.

Always use a rotary cutter on the kind of mat that is designed for it. Otherwise, it will quickly become dull and useless. To cut a strip of fabric, begin by ironing. Do not iron out the crease that goes down the middle of the fabric as it sits on the bolt. Fold the fabric in half along this crease and lay it over the cutting mat.

Using a straight edge (a wide, plastic cutting ruler made for this purpose works best) trim one vertical edge off the fabric. You will be cutting through two layers, but you will find that very little pressure is needed. Measure and cut your strips from this trimmed edge.

When all of the strips for squares are

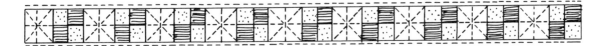

cut, you need to cut the wide strips for borders and the extra strips for binding and trim them to the correct length. Traditional tifaifai usually are not bound. Instead, the edges of the backing are folded to the front and sewn down over it. If you decide to do this, enlarge your backing fabric by 2″ all the way around and eliminate the binding strips.

After all the strips are cut out, measure and cut the strips for the mosaic pieces into exact squares. Use scissors, not the rotary cutter. (You will notice that the strip measurements in the following project are generous, leaving extra of each strip fabric for added squares if you make a mistake.) When the squares are cut, they will be 1½″ on each side. When they are sewn with a ¼″ seam allowance, each finished mosaic piece will be 1″ square.

Following the color-coded piecing diagram, join the squares into horizontal strips. In preparation for joining the squares, you can either lay out all of the pieces in their proper order (diagram style), or group your squares by color. The first will only work if you are lucky enough to have a room just for

your sewing that can be closed off to protect a partially sewn project. If you have pets or children with access to the same room the project is in, choose the color-grouping method. Just the thought of picking up those 324 squares after they have been inadvertently scattered may be enough to turn you off tifaifai forever.

When grouping squares by color, you may choose to string each color on a separate thread like the Tahitians do. As you join the squares into rows, the design does not look like much. But when the rows are joined together, the design will magically take shape. You will probably find that joining the tiny squares goes surprisingly quickly. Either hand or machine piecing is acceptable, although the Tahitians place a much higher value on hand-pieced tifaifai.

When the rows of squares are pieced, iron and lay out all rows in the proper order before joining them to each other. If you find, as you join the rows, that you have inverted a square or two, it is easy enough while still in this state to re-do them. When the design is pieced, you have only to add borders and binding to finish.

# ROSE WALL HANGING
Difficulty Level: Moderate

Please see Piecing and Binding in the chapter on Basic Techniques before beginning. See completed project in color section (Plate 7).

## MATERIALS

30″ wide square of backing fabric
Two 4″ × 22″ green border strips

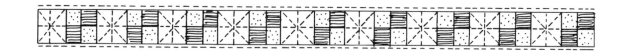

*Fig. 7-4. Rose Wall Hanging project.*

Two 4″ × 30″ green border strips
Four 2″ × 34″ bright green binding strips
Five 1½″ wide strips of black (A)
One ½″ wide strip of bright green (B)
Two 1½″ wide strips of green (G)
One 1½″ wide strip of dark green (D)
Two 1½″ wide strips of light pink (L)
Four 1½″ wide strips of medium pink (M)
Two 1½″ wide strips of purple-pink (P)
One 1½″ wide × 10″ long strip of yellow (X)
Note: All 1½″ wide design strips except black
   are 44/45″ long.

## DIRECTIONS

1. Cut all of the strips, setting aside the border and binding strips. Measure and cut the design strips into 1½″ squares.

2. Lay out the squares in the design pattern or organize them by color. Using the following diagram as a guide, piece the squares one horizontal row at a time.

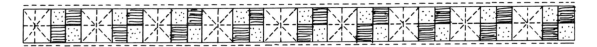

*Piecing Diagram*

Row 1: 2A, B, 3A, P, 2A, M, A, 2L, 5A.

Row 2: A, 3B, A, P, 2L, 2M, 3L, 5A.

Row 3: A, G, D, B, P, 3L, 2M, 3L, 3M, 2A.

Row 4: A, G, D, B, M, L, P, 2M, 3L, 4M, 2A.

Row 5: 2A, G, D, B, M, P, 2M, 3P, 4M, 2A.

Row 6: 2A, G, B, M, P, 2M, 5P, 2M, 3L.

Row 7: 3A, 2M, P, 2M, P, L, X, 3P, 3L, A.

Row 8: G, B, A, 2M, 2P, M, P, L, 2X, 2P, 3L, A.

Row 9: A, G, B, 3M, P, 2M, P, 2L, 2P, L, 2M, A.

Row 10: 2A, 2B, 2M, 3P, M, 3P, 4M, L.

Row 11: 5A, G, M, 2P, 6M, 2L, A.

Row 12: 4A, 2G, 2M, 3P, M, 2P, M, 3A.

Row 13: 3A, 2G, D, 4M, 2P, 3L, P, 2A.

Row 14: 2A, 2G, D, A, G, 6M, L, P, 3A.

Row 15: A, 2G, D, 2A, G, B, M, A, G, D, 2M, B, 3A.

Row 16: 2G, D, 4A, G, B, 2A, G, 2D, B, 3A.

Row 17: G, D, 5A, G, B, 3A, 2G, B, G, B, A.

Row 18: D, 7A, G, 9A.

3. When all rows are pieced, lay them out in the correct order. Check for mistakes and correct any squares that have been misplaced. Matching seams as you go, sew the rows together to form the design.

4. When the design is fully pieced, pin the two short border strips to the design square. Pin with right sides together, one on the left side of the design square, one on the right and sew. With right sides together, pin the two long border strips to the two remaining sides and sew in place to complete the border.

5. Place the design square with its completed border on the backing square with right sides facing out. Trim the backing square to the edges of the design square borders (unless you plan to bring the folded backing edges to the front for a finished edging).

6. Bind the edges using the green binding strips to complete the project.

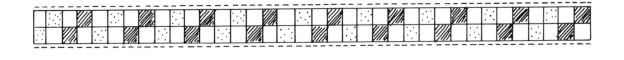

# Part Three: ASIA

# Chapter Eight

# Laos: Hmong Patchwork

# PATCHWORK: A REFUGE FOR REFUGEES

Tiny Laos is a country of hazy mountains, rice fields, Buddhist monasteries, and violent rains six months out of twelve. During the Vietnam War, U.S. planes routinely bombed the Ho Chi Minh Trail, a vital route through Laos for North Vietnamese supplies and troops. Now, after more than a decade of communist rule, this thinly populated, hilly nation, once known as "the Kingdom of a Million Elephants,"[1] is wrestling with its own version of *perestroika*. The Lao call it "chin tanakan may" or "new thinking." The signs of change are everywhere: people being released from re-education camps, land being returned to farmers, national elections (albeit within a one-party system), relaxed controls on foreign trade.[2] Reforms, however, come too late for one ethnic group, the Hmong (pronounced "mung"), the majority of whom have left the country or died defending their land.

The Hmong originally migrated from China to an unoccupied mountainous region between Laos and Vietnam during the 19th century. Here, they subsisted on unecological "slash-and-burn" agriculture, lived in isolated hamlets, and had little contact with the outside world. What contact there was usually took place when young men went to lowland markets to sell vegetables and buy items the mountain dwellers could not make for themselves.[3]

In their isolated refuge, life went on relatively peacefully for the Hmong until this century. Up until that point, they guarded their traditions and culture, worshipped their gods, and in the case of women, developed their own unique needlework style. Then, because their adopted homeland overlooked North Vietnam, the Hmong were inexorably drawn into the conflict that became the Vietnam War. They served as scouts and soldiers first for the French and later for the U.S. In doing so, they marked themselves for future retaliation. When the Americans withdrew in 1974, huge numbers of Hmong were forced to flee for their lives. Those who survived land mines, enemy gunfire, and hazardous jungle trails ended up in refugee camps in Thailand. Some of these traveled on to make their homes in the U.S., France, and Australia.

Today about 100,000 Hmong refugees make their home in America. Groups of Hmong refugee families are gathered in California, Wisconsin, Minnesota, Montana, and North Carolina. In recent years, they have tried to find settlement areas that reminded them of the hilly, verdant land they left behind.

For many Hmong, the transition to western culture has been difficult. It has involved the pain of racism and prejudice. But more than that, it represents a change in lifestyle so extreme that few of us who grew up here can begin to appreciate it. Things we take for granted like cars, locked doors, modern toilets, electric lights, even a written language, had no place in the traditional Hmong way of life but must be adapted to almost immediately upon arrival here.

In their homeland, the Hmong preserved their traditional ways. The elderly were respected for their wisdom and experience. Women kept to the roles of cooking, cleaning, and child-rearing. Land was plentiful and could be had (or at least farmed) for the clearing of it.

In America, the young ones are the quickest to learn English. They readily adapt to new ways, and take on the leadership role once enjoyed by older family members. Women are finding new freedom to work and attend school outside the home. In some cases, women are the main wage earners, selling their needlework. Land is seldom without its price and its use is regulated by law. In an attempt to hold onto something familiar, many urban-dwelling Hmong respond by hauling huge amounts of soil to create city gardens in unlikely places—swimming pools, living rooms, and narrow spaces between buildings. American eyes are startled to see such impromptu growing spaces flourishing with green mustard, cilantro, lemon cucumbers, and colorful flowering plants, but it is a bit of home to the Hmong refugees.

Through their gardens and through their needlework, many Hmong seek to preserve a part of their culture that is rapidly becoming lost amid the fast-paced American lifestyle. The traditional patchwork of the Hmong is called in their language Pa Ndau or "flower cloth." Like a perfect flower, it features color, symmetry and balance.

Hmong patchwork may feature geometric reverse appliqué, appliqué, embroidery, cross-stitch, or a combination of any of these (Fig. 8-1). No quilt stitching is used, although, as with quilts, the technique involves the use of three layers. In most pieces, a cut-out top fabric is appliquéd to a contrasting fabric with a lightweight foundation under it. Only solid strongly contrasting colors are used.

Hmong needlework is characterized by precise and practically invisible stitching. The infinitesimal appliqué stitches are close together and extremely fine, making the work beautiful as well as time-consuming.

Traditionally, Hmong patchwork was used to decorate clothing like belts, vests, and funeral garments, as well as some linens. Today, American consumers mostly encounter this craft in the form of pillows, wall hangings, vests, tablecloths, and shoulderbags. At large quilt shows, the decorated, ragged-edged patchwork squares are often a familiar sight, waiting to be finished into a desired item.

Lovers of Hmong patchwork fear that

*Fig. 8-1. Hmong patchwork.*

the technique itself could die out with its older and middle-aged practitioners since few young people take up this demanding and time-consuming form of needlework (Fig. 8-2). For the time being, though, the art of making "flower cloth" is in the capable hands of thousands of Laotian and Vietnamese refugees in their new homeland.

## NOTES

1. Peter T. White, "Laos Today," *National Geographic,* June 1987, p. 779.

2. "Lao Communists Do an About-Face," *U.S. News & World Report,* July 3, 1989, p. 35.

3. Carla Hassel, *Creating Pa Ndau Appliqué* (Lombard, IL: Wallace-Homestead Book Company, 1984), p. 6.

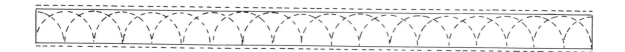

*Fig. 8-2. Hmong patchwork.*

# TECHNIQUES OF HMONG PATCHWORK

The most familiar form of Hmong needle-work is probably the geometric reverse appliqué square. Often surrounded by some version of a sawtooth border, it may feature a number of distinctive reverse appliqué elements that form a "star" or "snowflake" design. The basic elements that make up the larger designs go by names that sound appealingly exotic to American ears: Tiger's Eyebrow, Elephant's Foot, and Snailhouse, for instance. In some cases, the design elements symbolize ideas, although the symbolism does not appear to be universal. For one Hmong needlewoman the Snailhouse

may stand for eternal life. For another, it signifies family unity.

Less common, but also fairly often worked are embroideries (Plate 8). Colorful cotton embroidery pictures are created bearing the distinctive patchwork sawtooth border which marks them as items of Hmong origin. The embroidery pictures may tell a peaceful story of life in the verdant Laotian mountains or they may tell a perilous tale of escape from that dangerous land (Fig. 8-3).

In any item of reverse appliqué, a decorative top fabric is cut and turned under, leaving spaces through which a contrasting color of background fabric shows. Some people confuse the construction methods of Hmong patchwork and that of the reverse appliqué molas of the Cuna Indians of Panama (about which more is discussed in another chapter). Although both involve reverse appliqué and embroidery, the similarity ends there. Hmong patchwork usually features symmetrical geometric designs. It often includes a pieced triangular border. Molas today are often figurative although in the past more abstract geometrical

*Fig. 8-3. Hmong Needlework.*

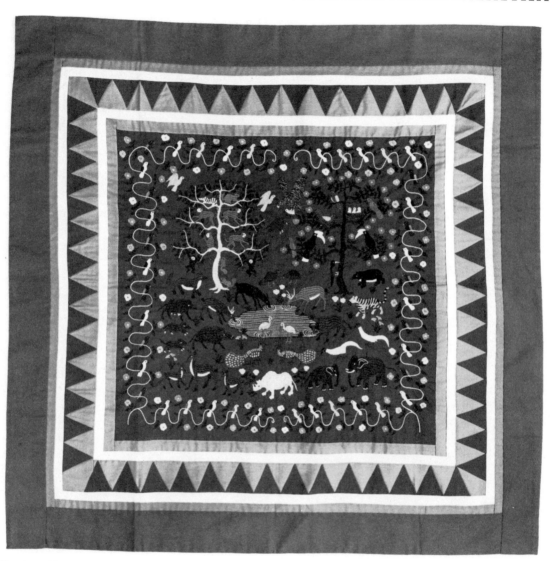

Fig. 8-4. Hmong Needlework.

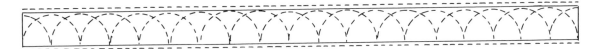

designs (though not necessarily symmetrical ones) were done. Molas do not include pieced borders.

The Hmong designs are worked from the top of the piece. The topmost fabric square is usually folded into a triangle that is folded once again to form a doubled triangle. The doubled triangle is basted to keep it from shifting and then the geometric elements are cut into the fabric. The design is built from front to back. It is cut into a top fabric which is appliquéd to an uncut colored fabric base and plain foundation fabric.

In the mola, fabric and appliqué layers are added from front to back and from back to front. The mola uses a combination of appliqué and reverse appliqué layers.

To achieve its precise symmetry, Hmong patchwork relies on a folded fabric technique similar in a way to Hawaiian quilting, but also unique. The folds are different and a piece may be folded, basted, and cut; then re-folded, re-basted, and cut again. The basting is necessary to keep the folded fabric from shifting while it is being cut. Even a tiny shift can throw off the intricate design.

Before tackling a Hmong-style reverse appliqué design it is best to try it out in paper first. Use motif and background fabrics that contrast strongly with each other (Plate 9). Hmong needleworkers usually cut their folded motif fabrics without drawing the design in, but you will probably want to use pencil lines as a guide. Sharp pointed embroidery or iris scissors work well for Hmong patchwork. Avoid scissors with large, blunt points. Usually, only a few short lines are cut into the folded and basted motif fabric as a guide. The rest of the cutting is done in stages after the motif fabric has been basted to the background. After a motif fabric is cut, and the basting removed, folding and ironing the creases of the motif fabric and the background fabric (as in Hawaiian quilting) will help with positioning the one on the other in preparation for appliquéing and additional cutting.

# CHRISTMAS STAR PILLOW   Difficult Level: Challenging

Please review Appliqué in the chapter on Basic Techniques before beginning. See completed project in color section (Plate 9, inset).

Be aware—despite its small size, this project is quite challenging. Hmong patchwork is noted for its intricacy and precision. This project is in the Star pattern, one of the easier designs for a newcomer to Pa Ndau to master.

Using red and green will provide good contrast. It also allows you to make this a Christmas project if you like. Or, substitute any other strongly contrasting colors.

Many Hmong pieces have a lightweight foundation fabric layer. For this sim-

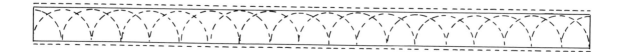

*Fig. 8-5. Hmong Christmas Star Pillow project.*

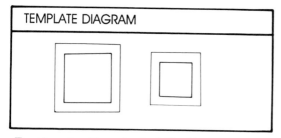

TEMPLATE DIAGRAM

*Templates for this project look like this and are found at the back of the book.*

ple project, you will omit this layer. More complex projects, however, should include a foundation to help stabilize a project while it is being sewn.

## MATERIALS

9½" square red cotton (motif)
11" square green cotton (background)
9½" square green backing fabric (pillow back)

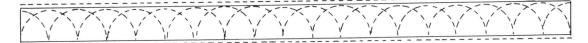

Scraps of black and green for corner
   squares and center square
Thread to match appliqués
Basting thread in contrasting color
Loose polyester filling

## DIRECTIONS

1. Fold the red square in half, then in half again, taking care to match the edges precisely. Then fold this smaller square along the diagonal. Baste the folded triangle you have made. Take plenty of $\frac{1}{2}''$ or so long basting stitches.

2. Hold the folded, basted triangle so that the long diagonal side is to the right and the center point (where all the folds would converge if you opened out the triangle) is at the bottom. Measuring away from this bottom point, mark a dot on the left side of the triangle at $1\frac{1}{2}''$, $2\frac{1}{2}''$, and $3\frac{1}{2}''$. Then, mark on the diagonal side also at $1\frac{1}{2}''$, $2\frac{1}{2}''$, and $3\frac{1}{2}''$. Cut a scant $\frac{1}{4}''$ snip at each mark you have made (Fig. 8-6). The cuts must be exactly perpendicular to the opposite folded side to form the star. Imagine that the opposite folded side is the cross-bar of a T and the cut you are making is the stem of the T. Keeping these cuts perpendicular to the opposite fold is important. You may want to practice on a piece of paper first just to get the idea.

3. Remove the basting stitches and open out the motif fabric. Fold it in half and in half again to make a square one quarter the

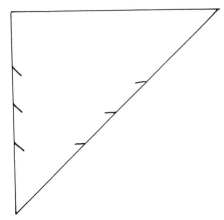

*Fig. 8-6. Cut a $\frac{1}{4}''$ snip at each mark you have made.*

size of the original square. Then iron the folds to find the center point. Do the same for the background fabric. (As in Hawaiian quilting, this folding technique allows you to find the exact middle of both motif and background fabric.) Then, using the ironed folds as a guide, position the motif fabric in the exact center of the background fabric and pin securely.

4. Run lines of basting through the ironed folds from top to bottom and from side to side. (Avoid basting where you can guess you will be turning under fabric to form the stars.) Next, run a straight line of basting from the top right corner to the bottom left corner; run another from the top left corner to the bottom right corner. You may want to mark the basting lines lightly in pencil before sewing since they will guide your final sewing. Finally, run one straight line of basting in the exact middle between each

line already sewn. These lines will be called mid-lines. Each one marks one inner angle between two star points. (You will have a total of sixteen basting lines running outward from the center, creating a symmetrical pattern of lines. Every other line will be a mid-line.) See Fig. 8-7.

5. For the centermost star, lightly, in pencil, extend the "lines" created by the snips you have made in the fabric to the point where they meet on the mid-line. Using this method, draw in the centermost star. Your pencil lines will join the eight points of the star (which are themselves marked by your snips in the motif fabric.) Cut along the first of the connecting lines you have drawn. The line you will be cutting lies in the

middle of a channel in the motif fabric. Through this channel, the background fabric will show. Therefore, cut only the motif fabric. Do not let the scissors point touch the background fabric. Cut only one drawn-in line. Clip the inward turning corner to enable you to turn under the fabric edge. Turn under and appliqué the edge of the inner star from one point, along the cut, to a second point. One at a time, do the same for each line you have drawn connecting two points. Clip inward-turning corners as needed. This will complete the appliquéing of the first inner star.

6. You will mark, cut, and sew each successive star in the same way. You will notice, however, that while the first star had only one side to be sewn, the following two stars are made by channels of background fabric showing through. So they have both an inner and outer outline of sewing. Where you stitched counterclockwise for the first star, begin the first round of sewing on star number two in a clockwise direction for greater ease. Then, for the second round of sewing on star number two, go back to a counterclockwise sewing direction. Repeat this procedure for star number three.

7. Appliqué the final star-shaped outline.

8. To embellish your sewn star, trace, mark fabric, and cut out five large squares from black fabric and five small squares from green fabric. Turn under each square. Position the green squares so that they are on

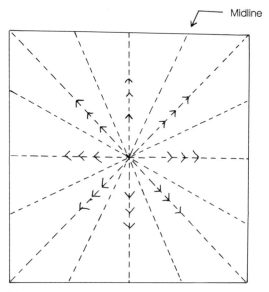

*Fig. 8-7. Example showing mid-line.*

point and appliqué each one to a black square. Then appliqué the black squares to the star center and the four corners.

9. Trim the background fabric to the size of the motif fabric (9½" square). With right sides together, sew the completed pillow front to the back all the way around the outside edge. Leave about 3" unsewn. Turn the pillow inside out. Stuff with polyester filling and sew the opening closed to complete the project.

# Chapter Nine

# Japan: Sashiko

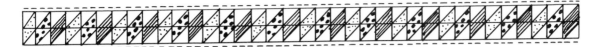

# MADE IN JAPAN

Two things impress the visitor upon seeing Japan—its mountains and its lush greenness. Mountains make up more than 85% of Japan's land area and the tallest of these, Mount Fuji, has inspired countless artists and artisans over the centuries. Outside the cities, mountainous terrain encompasses dramatic gorges, gushing waterfalls, and sparkling lakes. Farmland is at a premium and is terraced to produce the highest possible yields. Even so, with the dense population, much food must be imported. The land's striking natural features, because they limit urban expansion, are seen by some as Japan's greatest weakness, by others as its strength.

The Japanese have traditionally demonstrated a strong love of nature. The art of creating exquisite landscape gardens has been handed down for generations. Trees, shrubs, ponds, bridges, waterfalls, even stones and pebbles are carefully arranged to create a place conducive to meditation, a place where balance, proportion and harmony meet.

Coming from a tradition that values these qualities, it is not surprising that Japanese needlewomen have become strongly attracted to American quiltmaking. Today, schools in this transplanted craft flourish all over Japan. A look at the Japanese quilt magazine *Patchwork Quilt Tsushin* suggests what quilting means to many Japanese women today. Patience, endurance and precision are stressed.[1] A finely sewn quilt is an expression of these qualities in the maker. (Compare this to the emphasis in many American quilt magazines on how quickly a given project can be completed.)

Japanese women today make quilts to be hung on walls just as American women do. They also make *kotatsu* covers and futon covers. Many Japanese homes have little central heating in winter months. It is common for family members to seat themselves around a low table with a heater called a *kotatsu* over which a quilt is spread to keep in the warmth. In a traditional Japanese home, where bedding is rolled and stored away during the day, *kotatsu* covers enable women to put their quilting skills to use.

The padded futon, on which the modern Japanese sleep, is related (if distantly) to

*Fig. 9-1. Kyoto, Japan. Photograph courtesy of the Japan National Tourist Organization.*

our own western-style quilts. It is like a very thick, plain, channel-stitched or tied quilt stuffed with cotton. When not in use, it is rolled up and out of the way. To keep warm while sleeping on their futons, the Japanese draw over themselves a futon cover, also much like a quilt, but lighter in weight than the futon on which they sleep.

Japanese women today combine American quilting techniques, Japanese design elements, and antique Japanese fabrics to create masterpieces in piecing and appliqué. The basic techniques of patchwork, appliqué, and quilting, however, are not new to this region.

The oldest quilt known to exist was found in Asia. It was discovered in what is now the Soviet Union on the floor of a Scythian chieftain's tomb and dates from between 100 BC and 200 AD. It features cross-hatching and contour quilting, as well as finely detailed appliquéd animals.[2]

For centuries, Buddhist monks wore patched robes as a sign of poverty. But patchwork did not always denote want. It also embodied strong religious and social significance. Patched cloth was used to make religious articles including altar valances and hangings. Offerings of precious silk fragments were made by travelers at wayside temples on the Silk Road, the ancient trade route remarked upon by Marco Polo in his travels. Patchwork examples found in the Caves of the Thousand Buddhas included a large votive hanging, patchwork tops for banners, and a small silk

bag possibly used to contain relics. These bear a surprising resemblance to similar items made of Victorian crazy patchwork.[3]

In Japan, the sewing together of scraps from old textiles traditionally held symbolic meaning. In a sense, the needleworker was "prolonging" the life of the textiles of which only bits and pieces remained. A gift of patchwork consequently represented a wish for a prolonged life on the part of the recipient.

One form of patchwork known as *yosegire* or "sewing together of different fragments" was used for clothing, decorative cloths, or screens that served as partitions between sections of a room. Made up of randomly shaped patches, it recalls to mind the fabric shapes in American crazy patchwork, which it may have inspired during the late 1800s when an example of it was displayed in America.[4]

The Ainu, the original inhabitants of Japan, however, have a tradition of using cotton cloth to decorate their garments woven from elm-bark fibers. The appliqués were cut and sewn into twining maze or cable patterns and embroidered. The appliqué of the Ainu, however, was more than mere embellishment. It protected the wearer from evil and accident. It was therefore applied mainly to the more "vulnerable" garment areas such as cuffs, hem, neckline, and down the back along the spine.[5]

Strongly related to embroidery, sashiko (pronounced SAH-she-koh) is a whole cloth

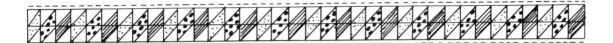

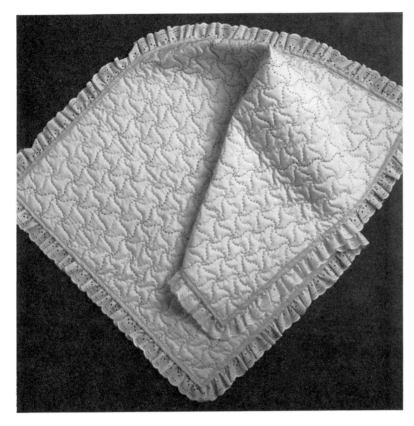

*Fig. 9-2. Crib quilt with sashiko stitching by Bonnie Benjamin of Needlearts International.*

technique of Japanese quilting. It is done on solid-colored fabric with multi-strand thread in a simple running stitch. Unlike traditional European/American quilting, sashiko usually has only four to six stitches per inch.

Sashiko originated in rural Japan about 300 years ago. The word sashiko means "little stabs." The origins of the technique are humble; it began as a means by which country folk sewed layers of cloth together to make thick, warm winter clothing. Sashiko was also used to make protective outerwear for firefighter's clothing. Drenched with water, heavy outer garments of sashiko-stitched fabric layers provided some defense against the heat and flames of a burning building.

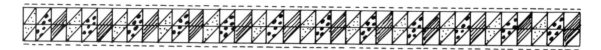

### NOTES

1. *Patchwork Quilt Tsushin*, number 28 (Tokyo: Patchwork Tsushin Co.), p. 8.

2. Jill Liddell and Yuko Watanabe, *Japanese Quilts* (New York: E.P. Dutton), p. 1.

3. Averil Colby, *Patchwork* (London: B.T. Batsford, 1976), p. 21.

4. Penny McMorris, *Crazy Quilts* (New York: E.P. Dutton, 1984), p. 12.

5. Schnuppe von Gwinner, *The History of the Patchwork Quilt* (West Chester, PA: 1988), pp. 43–44.

# TECHNIQUES OF SASHIKO

Traditionally, sashiko was done in white thread on fabric dyed dark indigo blue. Today, however, sashiko is done in many different colors on a variety of backgrounds. Most modern sashiko that is done in Japan uses only one layer of fabric. Many westerners practice sashiko quilting using a batting layer between two fabric layers, a development borrowed from their own quilting tradition. Unlike American quilting, however, a hoop or frame is not used in the quilting process.

Sashiko is a versatile technique that can be used in many ways. It can decorate cotton clothing or even garments made of very untraditional fabrics like velveteen or cotton knits. Sashiko with a batting layer makes beautiful vests, pillow tops, and wall hangings. The technique of sashiko stitching through a single fabric layer successfully produces decorative blouse yokes, skirt borders, sweatshirts, and shawls.

Careful marking is essential in neatly stitched sashiko. A pencil line may be necessary in marking complex traditional designs. For a simpler design like the one offered in this book, try using a quilter's tool known as a chalk wheel. Unlike a chalk pencil, the chalk wheel produces a fine line

*Fig. 9-3. Sashiko wall hanging by author.*

of loose chalk dust. The chalk does not work its way into the fabric; it rests on top of the fibers. Consequently it is easily brushed away when the project is completed.

Contrast is vital to a successful sashiko piece. The simple running stitch design should be done in light thread on dark fabric or dark thread on light fabric. Maintaining the same number of stitches per inch throughout the design is also important. Stitching should be done using a doubled thread and a large-eye embroidery needle.

The thread line should run in a continuous line as much as possible—avoid a lot of doubling back. The stitches should not be pulled tightly. Sewing so that the stitches on the front are slightly larger than on the back is fine.

The Japanese are well known for their paper-folding art of origami. What is perhaps less well known is that they also enjoy a needlework craft that involves joining folded fabric shapes. Squares, rectangles, octogons and other shapes are produced by

*Fig. 9-4. Wall hanging by Bonnie Benjamin of Needlearts International.*

folding fabric edges from back to front and creating mitered corners which are sewn down. These folded shapes may then be joined to others to produce heavy, un-quilted patchwork designs similar in con-struction to our own Cathedral Window pat-tern.

A large square done in Japanese folded patchwork technique forms the backing for the sashiko wall hanging described in the following project. In the case of a large fab-ric backing square, the edges are folded back to front, creating mitered corners. The miters may then be sewn or tacked down with the ragged fabric edge showing on the front of the piece. This makes a kind of soft fabric frame. A decorative square, such as that produced in the following sashiko project, is then centered and sewn down on the folded "frame" square. It should be po-sitioned so that it hides the ragged fabric edges showing on the front of the frame.

Japanese folded patchwork is not only suitable for backings for decorative wall hangings but also makes a great "patchwork as you go" technique. Entire quilts can be made of sewn patchwork squares joined to-gether, each with its own folded patchwork backing.

# SEASHELL WALL HANGING  Difficulty Level: Easy to Moderate

Please see Quilting in the chapter Basic Techniques before beginning. See com-pleted project in color section (Plate 10, top).

Before you begin, be sure to preshrink both the 100% cotton sashiko yarn and your fabric. This project uses a simple sashiko design that you can trace using a circle tem-plate. Be sure to divide the circle template into fourths and mark each fourth. This will enable you to mark the center design with its ovals and windows reminiscent of our own Wedding Ring pattern.

For more intricate designs and project ideas, please see Bonnie Benjamin's book, referenced in Recommended Reading. For sashiko yarn and other supplies, see Sup-plies and Suppliers.

## MATERIALS

30 gram skein crimson sashiko yarn
16" square of muslin top fabric (preferably 100% cotton)
16" square low-loft batting
16" square any color inner backing fabric (will not show)
26" square patterned "frame" outer backing fabric
Thread to match muslin and other backing fabric

*Fig. 9-5. Sashiko Wall Hanging project.*

## DIRECTIONS

1. Pre-shrink both sashiko yarn and fabric.

2. Measure and mark a 12″ square in the center of the 16″ muslin top fabric.

3. Trace the circular sashiko template (Fig. 9-6) onto cardboard and cut out. Mark the template into fourths as the example in the book is marked. Tracing around the template with a chalk wheel, mark the design onto the centered 12″ square in the middle of the muslin fabric (Fig. 9-7).

4. Place the top marked fabric right side up on the batting. Place both of these on the small 16″ inner backing fabric square with its right side down. Baste the three layers together.

5. To begin sewing use a doubled thread. Since the backing you are working with right now will not show, you can start your

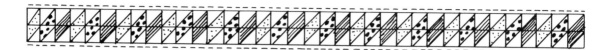

Sashiko
Quilting
Template

*Fig. 9-6. Circular template marked in fourths.*

thread with a knot. (Note: for single thickness layer sashiko, you would sew a few stitches in the opposite direction from the one in which you wanted to sew to anchor your thread.) Pull the knot through the backing fabric as you would in traditional American-style quilting. Sew in a continuous line, avoiding doubling back to complete a pattern line if possible. When you come to the end of your thread strand, make a knot close up against the back of the piece and pull the knot into the batting.

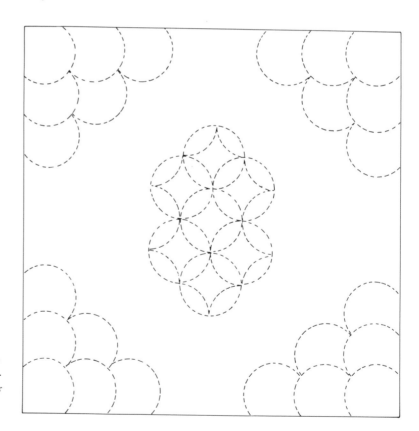

*Fig. 9-7. Fabric marked with circular template using four lines to determine positioning of circles.*

6. When you have completed sewing your sashiko design, trim the excess top fabric, batting, and inner backing fabric to make an even 12″ square with ½″ extra all the way around (13″ square total). Turn under the extra ½″ all the way around the sashiko-stitched square and baste in place. Set aside the completed square.

7. Fold the four sides of the large 26″ outer backing in toward the center. Fold in such a way that a miter is formed by the folds at each corner (Fig. 9-8). The frame produced on each folded side should measure 5″. (This will give your finished wall hanging a frame of 3″ with 2″ of the frame on each side tucked under the sashiko stitched square.)

8. Iron the folded outer backing. Sew the mitered corners down using an appliqué stitch and thread to match the fabric.

9. Center the basted sashiko-stitched square right side up on the folded outer

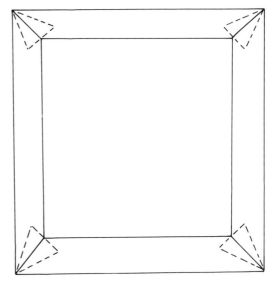

*Fig. 9-8. Example of mitered corners.*

backing. This will give you a 3″ frame of outer backing fabric all the way around. Pin the two pieces together. Then sew the sashiko-stitched square in place, using an appliqué stitch and thread to match the muslin to complete the project.

# Chapter Ten | India: Shisha Appliqué

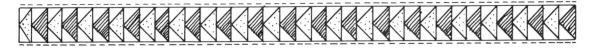

# MIRROR APPLIQUÉ: A REFLECTIVE ART

India is a land of extremes. The traveler witnesses scenes of poverty and images of almost unimaginable grandeur side by side. Want and disease are not hidden in the cities of Bombay, Calcutta, New Delhi. Westerners have had sulfone drugs at their disposal for decades. Here, many people still suffer from leprosy.

On the other hand are scenes of beauty—the Taj Mahal at Agra, a pearly

*Fig. 10-1. Faces of India. Photographed by John Forasté, Brown University.*

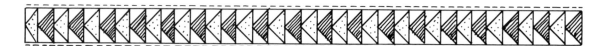

white monument to a loved one faced on one side by its mirror image in black marble; the ancient Elephant Caves and the stone path to them over which wild monkeys dance as if leading the visitor on; the swirling folds of a woman's sari that whorl gracefully as she walks. Miracles exist here too, in the homes and orphanages, for instance, begun by Mother Teresa. Her Home for the Destitute and Dying in Calcutta is just what its name implies. It is also a haven where dignity, warmth, and spiritual healing abide.

India has a long tradition of excellence in textile and needlework design. Historically, Indian quilts and fabrics had a strong influence on European quiltmaking, especially in England. The English East India Trade company was formed in 1600. The resulting trade with India is cited by one researcher as an important factor in the rising popularity of quilting in seventeenth century England.[1] From India came cotton-filled quilts in designs that must have appeared exotic to British eyes. Indian palampores and hand-printed and painted chintz were also imported. The knowledge and color management that India textile workers displayed was unknown in the west and consequently textiles and quilts imported from that country were eagerly sought after by fashionable British citizens.

Today, quilts are still made in India. Among the ethnic group known as the Jat, for instance, who live in northern areas of the country, patchwork quilts often form an important part of a woman's dowry. Pieced squares may be arranged in a pattern much like the Amish Sunshine and Shadow design and quilted with black or red thread. Finished quilts are stored in the home in patchwork bags and the number of quilts owned by a household gives an indication of the family's status within a community.

Typically, quilts among the Jat are made from fabric scraps saved from old clothing. For these women, the act of sewing a useful quilt from worn out clothing is symbolic of a kind of reawakening. Something new and lively is created from that which was old and "dead."[2]

In warmer regions, featherlight cotton gauze quilts without batting are used. Made either of whole cloth printed in striking paisley patterns, or colorful pieced work, these are often basted, quilt top to backing fabric, with large, loose $\frac{1}{2}''$ stitches done in regular sewing thread. Travelers often carry such versatile, lightweight quilts. On a journey they can be used to provide warmth depending on the season. They offer a degree of personal privacy when used as a cover-up. Or, folded, they make a soft pillow.

A kind of embroidery similar to quilting is traditionally made in Lucknow. Lucknowi work is often used to decorate clothing and features precise handstitching on a solid colored fabric. Breathtakingly even, the stitches are about $\frac{1}{8}''$ in length and trace out softly curving paisley designs. A cotton thread thicker than our own quilting thread, yet thinner than perle cotton or embroidery floss is used.

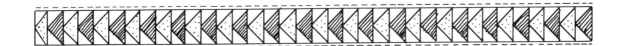

*Fig. 10-2. Quilted food cover* (atree) *from the Kutch region of India. Photograph courtesy of The Fowler Museum of Cultural History, University of California.*

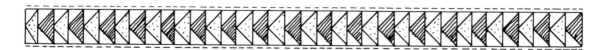

*Fig. 10-3. Shisha shawl.*

In both India and Pakistan, an appliqué technique is used in which little mirrors are applied to a fabric backing (Fig. 10-3). The mirrors are called "shishas" and the technique, known as shisha appliqué, mirror appliqué, or mirror embroidery is used to decorate shawls, dress bodices, sleeves and hems, purses and other fabric items. At one time this technique was done using real glass mirrors. Evil spirits or "jinns" were believed to be frightened away by seeing their own faces in the tiny mirrors.[3] Today, the mirrors are often made of metal or cardboard-backed aluminum. They are anchored on a background fabric using a blanket stitch, usually in a single color of cotton embroidery thread (see color section (Plate 11).

## NOTES

1. Dorothy Osler, *Traditional British Quilts* (London: B.T. Batsford, 1987), p. 87.

2. Schnuppe von Gwinner, *The History of the Patchwork Quilt* (West Chester, PA: Schiffer Publishing, 1988), pp. 33, 37.

3. Marie-Janine Solvit, *The Art of Appliqué* (New York: Arco Publishing, 1984), p. 15.

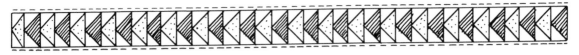

# TECHNIQUES OF SHISHA APPLIQUÉ

Various sizes of mirror chips for use in shisha appliqué can be obtained at craft stores. Actual Indian shishas are usually about ½″ in diameter. Antique shishas were sometimes even smaller. You may find circular mirror chips as large as 1″ in diameter at American craft shops. Failing real mirror chips, you can use Mylar (a shiny aluminum with fabric backing available at art supply stores), or wrap tiny cardboard circles with heavy duty aluminum foil.

In India, shishas are usually sewn onto solid hand-dyed cloth. You too, will want to choose a solid color for your shisha backing fabric so as not to detract from the design created by the tiny mirrors and the decorative embroidery stitches that secure them. The shisha can be gently held in place with a dab of glue while you sew it down. Do not use so much glue, however, that it seeps beyond the edge of the shisha into the area of the background fabric which is to be sewn (Fig. 10-5).

A shisha is sewn into place using a criss-cross of stitches like a tic-tac-toe grid (Fig. 10-6). Take two parallel stitches from top to

*Fig. 10-4. Two purses decorated with shisha appliqué.*

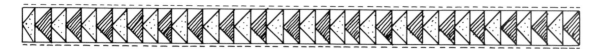

*Fig. 10-5. Shisha shawl show-
ing detail of stitches.*

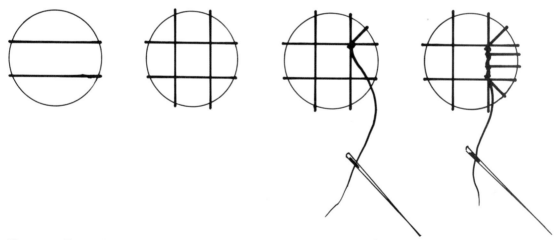

*Fig. 10-6. Example of criss-cross stitches over shishas.*

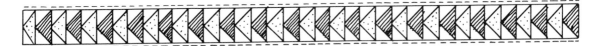

bottom. Add two more parallel stitches from side to side to complete the initial grid. Using the grid as a base, add stitches from the outer rim of the shisha to the center square of the grid. Usually a buttonhole stitch is used.

# MIRRORED SLEEVE BORDERS
### Difficulty Level: Easy to Moderate

See completed project in color section (Plate 3).

Use shisha appliqué to make a narrow band for decorating the sleeves of a blouse. Since blouse sleeve sizes vary, no exact measurements will be given for this project.

## MATERIALS

Large 1" diameter circular mirrors
2" wide solid cotton shisha fabric backing strip
Assorted fabric strips each 1" wide for decorating shisha backing strip
Glue stick or craft glue
Embroidery floss
Embroidery needle
Thread for appliquéing shisha strip to blouse sleeve

## DIRECTIONS

1. You will be making two shisha sleeve borders, one for each sleeve. For each border, use the following method. Measure the sleeve of the blouse that is to receive the shisha border. Mark the strip with pencil to indicate where each tiny mirror is to fall. Use a very small dab of glue to assist your fingers in holding the mirror in place while you sew.

*Fig. 10-7. Detail of Sleeve Borders project.*

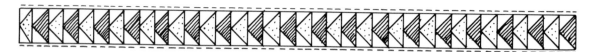

2. Double your embroidery thread and knot it. You will work from the front of the piece as you sew. Holding the first glued shisha in place on the fabric backing with your fingers, sew first one stitch, then another parallel to it over the mirror from top to bottom. You will be bringing the thread out through the fabric backing at the mirror top, running it over the mirror and returning it into the fabric backing at the mirror bottom. Do similar parallel stitches from side to side to produce a tic-tac-toe type of grid over the mirror. Add on blanket stitches around the tic-tac-toe grid to form it into a circle.

3. Secure the remaining shishas with embroidery stitches as you did the first one.

4. By machine or hand sewing, join the assorted strips to each other to make two decorative bands. (See the project sample if you need help.) Then sew the strip bands, one on either side, to the shisha-stitched fabric backing.

5. Sew the second shisha sleeve border as you did the first. Appliqué both to the sleeves of the blouse.

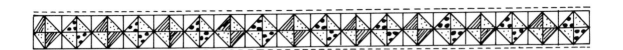

# Part Four: AFRICA

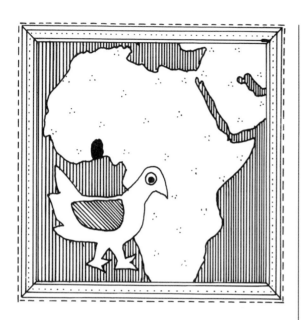

# Chapter Eleven | African Appliqué

# WARRIOR QUILTS

"How keenly the human mind yearns for geometrical figures," wrote Isak Dineson.[1] In an observation that could have been made by any quilter, she expressed her reaction to "the wildness and irregularity" of the African landscape she saw in contrast to her neatly laid out farm. Africa is a continent of staggering diversity—of many different terrains, peoples, customs, and religions.

The scent of woodsmoke mixed with cooking peanut oil; walkways of bare, packed earth; red clay homes with thatched roofs and iron cooking pots in front are images that greet the visitor to West Africa. In the marketplace, the women spread their wares on rattan mats. Pots burnished with indigo, gaudy enamelware from China, brass lamps, leather goods, fabric made from narrow sewn-together woven strips abound. The food sold consists of different kinds of yams in all shapes and sizes, cooking oil, corn, canned tomatoes from Italy, onions, bags of rice and peanuts. Here too one might find for sale colorful modern appliquéd banners, descendents of the ancient ceremonial banners of the Fon people.

Centuries ago, the Fon of West Africa developed the art of making appliquéd cloth. But where we think of appliqué (just as we do quilting techniques in general) as part of a warm, protective, nurturing tradition, there was nothing warm or protective about *these* appliqués. In a warrior culture, they provided a symbolic means for recording the deeds of battles, executions, and the legendary power of fierce kings.

In Dahomey (now known as Benin), appliquéd cloth was traditionally used for ceremonial banners, ritual clothing, state umbrellas, and was displayed by people of rank. Symbolic figures of people and animals were cut from brightly colored cloth

*Fig. 11-1. Two girls of West Africa. Photograph by David Sacco.*

and sewn onto a backing of black, gold, or white fabric. The animal images were often used to suggest a leader's strength or war-like capabilities.

Part of an oral tradition, the banners involved a kind of picture writing that was generally understood by the community.

The symbolic message was often reinforced by accompanying songs. Important chiefs and warriors recorded their deeds on white umbrellas given to them by the king. These umbrellas have been seen as fulfilling a similar role to the heraldic banners of European nobles.

# TECHNIQUES OF AFRICAN APPLIQUÉ

Appliquéd cloth and the rituals which surrounded it was important as an instrument by which leaders retained their leadership role. Consequently, the production of appliquéd cloth was strictly regulated. It was produced by men and only by members of the court tailor's guild. The families of these craftsmen enjoyed great status as a result of their association with royal clients.[2]

When the Portuguese arrived in West Africa in the fifteenth century, they found a prosperous, well-organized civilization. In 1486, Affonso d'Aveiro and his band of traders purchased the first pepper to reach Europe from West Africa. Before long, the Portuguese were also purchasing slaves. Slavery had been going on in Africa for centuries, but with the Portuguese began the first large-scale export of black Africans from their homeland.

Early visitors and explorers to the capital city of Abomey were impressed by the wealth and evidence of culture they found there. They treated the African rulers with the same deference they would have shown a European head of state. But something changed over the intervening centuries.

The first Portuguese arrivals to this territory were portrayed in bronze plaques cast by their African hosts. When the plaques were removed to England in 1897, however, no one would believe they were of African origin. It was decided that the Portuguese had taught their hosts the art of bronze casting. Since then it has been established that the natives were casting bronze long before the Europeans arrived.

Although the Portuguese were the first Europeans to explore this area, it was the French who were to exercise the most lasting western influence. During the 19th century, Africa became a stage for the European powers to grab whatever they could. In effect, the whole continent was divided up

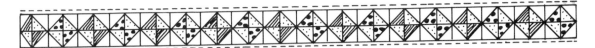

*Fig. 11-2. Appliquéd Asante asafo flag, Ghana. Photograph courtesy of The Fowler Museum of Cultural History, University of California.*

by the British, French, Belgians and Portuguese. European-established boundaries took little notice of tribal allegiances (which is one reason some African states today have difficulty with unification). The territory that had included Dahomey was made a French protectorate and in 1902 became part of the Federation of French West Africa.

Independence came to most French colonies in 1960. The next decade or so

brought a succession of violent power struggles in Dahomey, ending with a coup in 1972 by communist leader Major Kerekou. In an effort to remove any taint of colonialism, Dahomey changed its name to Benin in 1975.

Under the French, the court tailors of the Fon continued to make their appliqué banners, umbrellas and other ceremonial objects. They no longer recorded contemporary conquests, however, but told a story

of past grandeur. In time, the themes of the appliqués changed. Modern appliqués retain some of the old figures and are made more or less using the same techniques. Banners are not as large as they once were, and a wider color range is used.

Other West African tribes also practiced the making of ceremonial appliqué. Flags or banners, often with war-like themes, were made by the Asante of Ghana. Examples often feature figures of men with guns. The Anang-Ibibio people of Nigeria made appliquéd burial clothes depicting the life of their dead. The banners were displayed at a funeral, their story "read" by family members, and then abandoned to the ravages of wind, rain, and time—which explains why no old examples have survived.

In the United States, the figures of two famous Bible quilts have given rise to the speculation that their maker, Harriet Powers, may have been influenced by Dahomian appliqués. Harriet Powers was born a slave in Georgia in 1837. After the Civil War, she and her husband established a small farm near Athens, Georgia. She lived in this area until her death in 1911. Only two of her quilts are known to exist (Fig. 11-3). Both are executed in appliqué technique and depict Bible and other scenes of religious significance to her.

In contrast to many delicate "western" appliqués of the same period, Harriet Powers' figures display the "chunky", strong, exuberant qualities that are unique to West African appliqué. Whether Mrs. Powers was influenced by West African appliqués is still

a question. Many slaves came from West Africa, but, as one researcher points out: "By the time her parents' generation would have come to the South, most slaves were being imported from the Congo and Angola. Even if they came from West Africa . . . they would not necessarily be knowledgeable in the appliqué techniques. . . . It seems most likely that she could have acquired a knowledge of African style by hearsay from other, older house slaves or from her parents, or other older persons."[3]

Today, interest in Afro-American quilts is steadily growing. Many of these quilts are based on strip patterns. Researchers have drawn attention to the relationship between contemporary African-American strip quilts and the traditional African strip woven fabrics of West Africa. West African men weave fabric on looms as narrow as 4″ wide. The resulting strips are sewn together into large textiles which may then be sewn into clothing or household furnishings. In many cases, African-American quilters adapted American block style patterns to the strip-design, reflecting their own African-inspired aesthetic.[4]

In African textiles, woven strips can be aligned to create symmetrical designs, but are more often joined in such a way that asymmetrical designs are produced. The result is an intentional scattering of color over an entire piece. The same kind of asymmetrical patterning is found in many African-American quilts, according to art professor Maude Wahlman. "Another characteristic that you find in African textiles and in Afro-

*Fig. 11-3. Appliqué quilt made by Harriet Powers of Athens, Georgia, c.1895. This quilt by an African-American bears strong resemblance to the appliqué work of West African artisans. Photograph courtesy of The Smithsonian Institution, Washington, D.C.*

American quilts is the emphasis on bright contrasting colors. The reason for this in Africa is that in order to be read from a distance in the bright sunlight, cloth has to be bright."[5]

Are many of us negatively biased by British/American quilting standards? Some scholars think so. A ground-breaking exhibit was organized by collector Eli Leon in 1988 at the San Francisco Art and Craft Museum

African Appliqué **127**

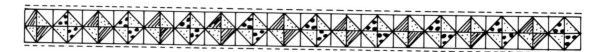

*Fig. 11-4. Double Strip quilt by Alberta Collins, c.1943. The strip construction of this African-American quilt is suggestive of strip-pieced fabrics typical of West Africa. Photograph courtesy of the San Francisco Craft & Folk Art Museum.*

titled "Who'd A Thought It: Improvisation in African-American Quiltmaking." In it, the public was encouraged to look at quilts in a new way. In the past, the irregular patterns of many African-American quilts had been perceived as mistakes. The fault, suggested Leon, was not with the quilts but with the (in this instance) inappropriate standards by which they were being viewed. For the first time, these irregularities of color and pattern came to be seen not as an absence of symmetry, but as products of a distinctive African-American aesthetic of improvisation. The message was clear: just as improvisation is important to jazz and other African-inspired musical forms, so is it important to the visual art of African-American quilts.[6] Leon has further suggested that patchwork itself may have originated in Africa rather than Asia, as many researchers have hypothesized. In any case, we still have much to learn from and about the tradition of West African appliqué and its descendant African-American patchwork.

## NOTES

1. Isak Dineson, *Isak Dineson's Africa: Images of the Wild Continent from the Writer's Life and Words* (San Francisco: Sierra Club Books, 1985), p. 40.

2. Schnuppe von Gwinner, *The History of the Patchwork Quilt* (West Chester, PA: Schiffer Publishing Company, 1988), p. 29.

3. Dr. Monni Adams, "Harriet Powers' Bible Quilts," *The Clarion* (Spring 1982, The Museum of American Folk Art, New York City), p. 43.

4. Barbara Brackman, "The Strip Tradition in European-American Quilts," *The Clarion* (Fall 1989, The Museum of American Folk Art, New York City), p. 45.

5. Maude Wahlman, quoted in *Quilting II*, with Penny McMorris, a guide to accompany the

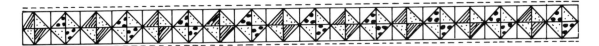

television series produced by WBGU-TV (Bowling Green, KY: Bowling Green State University, 1982), p. 56.

6. Eli Leon, *Who'd A Thought It*, catalog to the exhibition held from December 31, 1987 to February 28, 1988 at the San Francisco Craft and Folk Art Museum, p. 22.

# DAHOMEY-STYLE APPLIQUÉ BANNER
## Difficulty Level: Easy to Moderate

Please review Appliqué and Binding in the chapter on Basic Techniques before beginning. See completed project in color section (Plate 12).

## SUGGESTED VARIATIONS

Traditional West African appliqué was done in solid colored cottons. Try sewing cotton appliqués on velveteen or other rich fabric and decorating with gold thread and other embroidery.

## MATERIALS

19" × 31" rectangle solid black cotton
Five "fat" quarters bright solid cottons: red, blue, green, purple, magenta
Four fabric strips 1½" wide × 1 yard long in black or an appliqué fabric
Thread to match appliqué fabrics

## DIRECTIONS

1. To make templates, photocopy or trace the patterns for the appliqués. Or, plan to cut your appliqué figures freehand for a more animated look. See Fig. 11-6 for additional appliqué figures.

2. Mark the appliqué patterns on the fabric and cut out. Allow ¼" all the way around

*Fig. 11-5. Dahomey-Style Appliqué Banner project.*

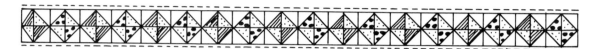

## TEMPLATE DIAGRAM

*Templates for this project look like this and are found at the back of the book.*

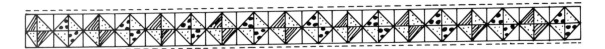

## TEMPLATE DIAGRAM (continued)

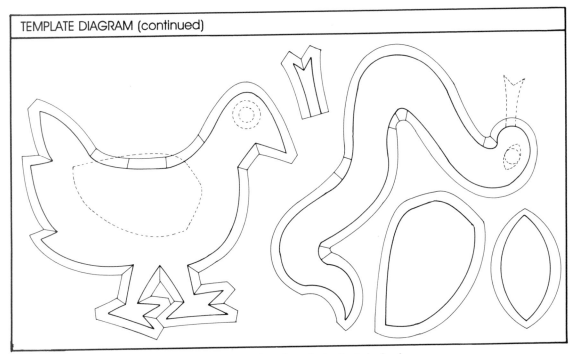

*Templates for this project look like this and are found at the back of the book.*

*Fig. 11-6. Additional figures for appliqué.*

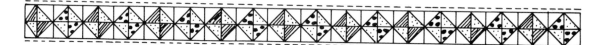

each appliqué for turning under. Iron the cut outs. Clip around the inward-turning curves and into corners up to, but not into the fold line of the appliqués.

3. Position and pin the large base appliqué shapes on the background fabric. Set aside the smaller decorative appliqués. See the project sample for help in positioning. Allow no more than 1½" of space at the edges of the background fabric.

4. Sew the large, base shape appliqués in place using matching thread and an appliqué stitch.

5. Sew the smaller decorative appliqués on top of the base shapes. Take care to stitch through all layers of fabric.

6. Trim the ragged edge of the background fabric with thin fabric strips made from black cotton or from one of the appliqué fabrics. Sew loops at the top for hanging if desired.

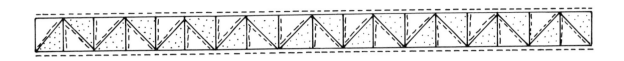

# Part Five: EUROPE

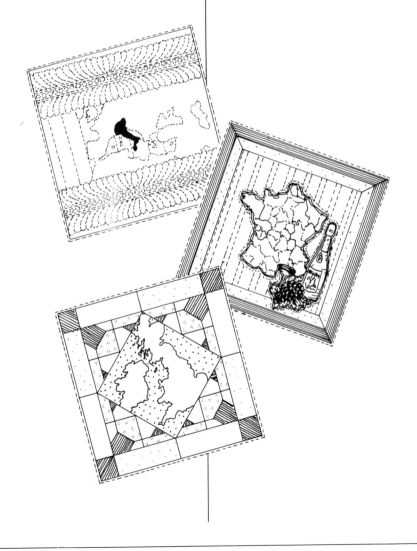

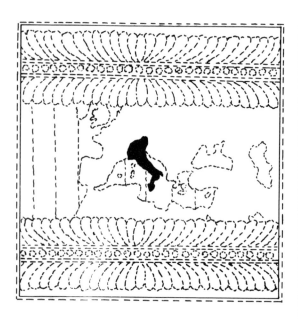

# Chapter Twelve | Italy: Trapunto

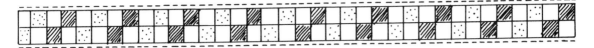

# A RENAISSANCE OF QUILTMAKING

Looking out across the red tiled roofs of Florence, Italy, the eye embraces a panorama of angles and archways in stone. An ancient scene, it reminds one curiously of contemporary abstract patchwork.

Beneath the shadow of the Duomo, the visitor to Florence can observe some of the world's greatest art treasures: Michelangelos' *David*, Ghiberti's bronze doors, *The Gates of Paradise*, Botticelli's *Birth of Venus* (Fig. 12-1). Yet, that which is most compelling about Florence can only be savored by walking its stone streets. It is the sound of church bells in the morning, the sun on the fruit seller's stall piled high with ripe peaches, the scent of the woodcarver's studio, the street lanterns reflected by night in the muddy Arno.

The city harbors some delightful surprises for quilters. Workers of pieced fabric quilts can appreciate the complex stone mosaics of the Baptistry floor in a way no one else can. Here, as in many of Italy's old churches, artisans created in colored marble the patterns we have come to know as Tumbling Blocks, Flying Geese, and Broken Dishes. To walk around the inside is almost like committing the sacrilege of marching over quilts and makes a quilter feel oddly guilty. Worn uneven by the tread of generations, these colorful patterns are patchwork in stone. (Even if you cannot take a trip to Florence to enjoy the floor mosaics just now, you can enjoy taking a look at Helen Fairfield's *Patchwork from Mosaics* which includes more than 100 designs for patchwork from Italian stone floors.)

Coming from a vast pieced work tradition, American quilters may be surprised at the lack of a similar fabric tradition in Italy. We must remember that our tradition, like our nation, is young. To us, a quilt is old if it dates from the early 1800s. Here "old" can commonly mean anything from the 11th or 12th century or earlier. To find evidence of patchwork as it was used by the ancient Florentines, we must know where to look. During the Middle Ages, cloth hangings were often used to decorate walls. While many of these were loomed tapestries, some would seem to have been made of pieced fabric. No actual garments or furnishings

*Fig. 12-1. View of Florence and the Duomo.*

have survived, but we can guess that patchwork was done during this time from its appearance in artwork of the times.

One fresco of special interest to quilters is in the Basilica of Santa Croce. Painted by Taddeo Gaddi, a student of Giotto, it is in the Baroncelli Chapel to the right of the altar. The scene portrays the wedding of the virgin (Fig. 12-2). Behind the Bride's head is draped a magnificent wall hanging. The draping at the top of the hanging indicates a soft, fabric composition. The brilliant colors and sharp edges of the pattern suggest pieced fabric construction. The pattern is made up of stars in green and gold, connected by small white squares and crimson pentagons, an enviable pattern by any quilter's standards.

With so much inspiring beauty to draw upon, it is disappointing to reflect that the Italians have no true word for "quilt." The closest in meaning is the word *coperte*, simi-

*Fig. 12-2. "The Wedding of the Virgin" by Taddeo Gaddi, 14th century, from the Baroncelli Chapel, Santa Croce, Florence, Italy.*

lar to "coverlet," or "trapunto" which refers to the technique often used in decorating a coverlet. Trapunto is a form of stuffed quilting traditionally done in Italy. It does not make use of patchwork or appliqué. Instead, graceful, fluid designs often featuring flowers, fruits and vines, are drawn on white linen. These are quilted with outline stitching to a loosely woven backing which is then opened to allow bits of stuffing to pad the individual design elements.

The Palazzo Davanzati was built around the middle of the 14th century. Today it houses the collection of the Museo della Casa Fiorentina Antica, the Museum of the Ancient Florentine Home. Painted wooden chests, antique laces, intricately carved cupboards, colorful ceramics and other household items made between the 14th and 17th centuries are handsomely displayed. For a quilter, however, the treasure of the collection is a linen bedspread featuring scenes from the life of the legendary knight Tristram done in trapunto or stuffed quilting (Fig. 12-3). A portion of the quilt is displayed here while a remaining portion is in the collection of the Victoria and Albert Museum in London.

Scholars remark on the outstanding preservation of this bed covering. Quilters are inclined more to remark on the intensity of labor to which it bears witness. The coverlet is crowded with dramatic figures of quilted knights and princes, sophisticated ladies, and trumpet-sounding heralds. Completing the pictures are twining vines, decorative leaves and gothic lettering in a

*Fig. 12-3. Detail of Sicilian trapunto bed covering portraying the Tristram legend, c.1395. The scene depicts King Languis sitting on a throne in front of his castle giving a letter to two kneeling ambassadors while three nobles stand in attendance behind him. Photograph courtesy of the Victoria and Albert Museum.*

tantalizingly obscure Sicilian dialect. The quilt was probably the product of a trapunto workshop run by male artisans, rather than the work of a single woman.

Trapunto involves two main techniques of stuffing. The first of these, usually called "trapunto," involves stuffing loose filling into an area enclosed by stitching.

The stuffing is inserted through a hole in the backing fabric. The second is called "cording," or "Italian quilting." In this method, two parallel lines of quilting are sewn with a small passageway between them. Through this passageway, a cord or length of yarn is pulled, creating a neat, raised pattern line.

Both kinds of trapunto work (stuffed work and cording) require a top fabric and a bottom fabric. Interestingly, this kind of quilting did not develop with a third "batting" layer in between, probably because it originated in warmer regions. Trapunto is believed to have first developed in sunny Sicily (the origin of the Tristram quilt of the Palazzo Davanzati) where the climate did not demand heavy quilted fashions.

In the 14th century, when this coverlet was made, the bed was appropriately regarded as a very important piece of furniture. In it, life began and ended. Custom of the times paid homage to such importance, it being common for the lady of the house to receive her friends seated on her bed.[1] This habit, of course, encouraged the creation of outrageously ornate bed coverings such as the highly detailed "Tristram quilt."

Trapunto and regular quilting was also used in clothing during this time, particularly in armor. Evidence from inventories and other records indicates that quilted jackets and vests were worn as a form of protection. Some contained small metal plates in addition to stuffing, providing substantial defence in the days when weapons were largely limited to daggers, arrows, swords, and spears. Of course, with the advent of firearms, protective quilted outerwear was no longer as useful for self-defense as it once had been.

Stuffed quilting was probably common in more everyday clothing as well. That this is possible is suggested by an ivory carving of the Flight into Egypt, made in Milan, Italy about 1400, now in the Victoria and Albert Museum in England. The carving depicts Joseph wearing a coat quilted in cross hatching. It has been suggested that this little carved figure with his quilted coat may have been inspired by the everyday dress of a real Italian peasant of the day.[2]

Far from diminishing in popularity as a technique for sewing bed coverings and clothing, stuffed quilting seems to have become even more fashionable with succeeding generations. It was especially popular throughout Western Europe in the 16th and 17th centuries as clothing decoration. Or perhaps we just have more surviving pieces from later periods to draw upon. In any case, trapunto techniques were kept alive from these early days of Florentine wealth and prominence well into our own time.

## NOTES

1. Todorow, Maria Fossi, ed., *Palazzo Davanzati* (Florence: Italy, "Lo Studiolo," 1986), p. 18.

2. Averil Colby, *Quilting* (New York: Charles Scribner's Sons, 1971), pp. 8–9, pp. 16–18.

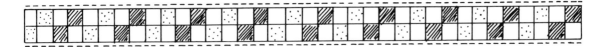

# TECHNIQUES OF TRAPUNTO

Many modern fabric artists recognize the added spark that stuffed quilting can give to a design. Trapunto can be especially successful in a wide variety of contexts. Stuffed quilting can be used with shiny, one-color fabrics like satin or polished cotton to create a tactile design that almost begs the viewer's touch. It can be used to embellish printed fabric designs, causing individual flowers and leaves to stand out in a large floral print. Trapunto can also be used to enhance the center square of a patchwork or strip-pieced medallion quilt (see Plate 13 in color section).

The top fabric in trapunto should be of fairly tight weave so as to hold in the stuffing. It should not be so stiffly woven, however, that it lacks "give." The give in a fabric is what brings out the design with all its dramatic "hills" and "valleys" of light and shadow. The right kind of fabric (usually cotton, linen, or satin) can provide plenty of contrast, even for one-color projects.

The bottom fabric, to which the top one is stitched, may be looser or less tightly woven. In stuffed quilting especially, it should be loose enough to facilitate being cut open or having its threads separated to admit the stuffing.

Historically, a variety of stitches were used in trapunto. The most common today are a running stitch, like the kind used in regular quilting, or a back stitch, like that often used to reinforce hand-sewn seams in clothing. The back stitch is done from the top of the work and is a bit more time-consuming. It is easier, however, for those who have trouble maintaining tight, even stitches. The running stitch, done with about six to eight stitches per inch is also appropriate. In this method the design may be drawn on the back of the work and sewn from the back, leaving no tell-tale lines on the front. As in normal quilting, the quantity of stitches in either technique is less important than their evenness.

Using a hoop to sew trapunto will keep the work from shifting. When using a hoop, keep in mind that your trapunto design, hardly apparent when the project is in the hoop, will be much more dramatic when the work is removed. If you do not use a hoop, either because a project is too small, or because you just do not feel comfortable with one, you will need to smooth the fabric constantly as you work. This keeps puckers from forming.

Unless you are experimenting with a special effect, the thread should match the top fabric of your project. This way it will not detract from the raised effect of the design. Regular thread is fine for smaller projects that will not receive wear. Quilting thread is best for larger projects. A thimble is important in any kind of quilting.

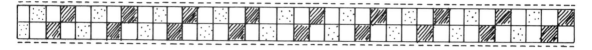

*Fig. 12-4. Border detail of trapunto coverlet by Luci Foote of Colchester, Connecticut, c.1816. Photograph courtesy of the Stamford Historical Society.*

To do the stuffing, the back may have a small slit cut into it, a procedure known as "cut-back" stuffing. Or, the back may have its threads pulled open gently in a technique known as open-weave stuffing. To cut the backing, tiny sharp surgical scissors are used. The polyester filling is introduced through the slit. A popsicle stick works well for pushing the stuffing into place. The slit is then sewn closed using large basting stitches.

To open the threads and avoid having to cut the backing, a number of tools can be used. A wooden stick may be sharpened to a point and smoothed with sandpaper or a Victorian sewing awl may be used. Made from vegetable ivory, this tool can sometimes be found at antique shops and flea

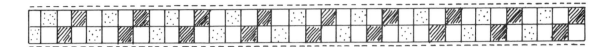

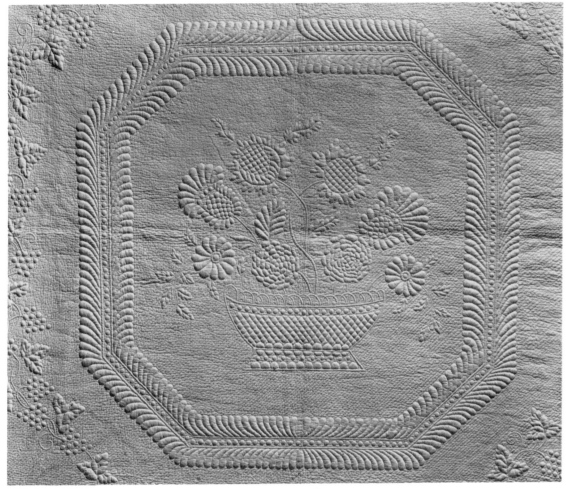

*Fig. 12-5. Center detail of trapunto coverlet made by Lucy Foote.*

markets. It is very effective in working apart threads and closing them together again after the stuffing is done.

For cording, use a plastic yarn needle or large blunt tapestry needle and synthetic yarn. The yarn may be doubled according to the thickness of the passageway between the parallel lines of quilting that is being filled. Work the needle into the passageway from the back and pull the yarn through.

The needle is brought out when it has gone as far as it can without twisting the fabric. It is then reinserted into the same hole it came out of. When the time comes to cut the cord, it should not be knotted. Instead, a length of yarn about ½″ long is left dangling on the outside back of the project. This allows for give within a piece. If two cording passageways cross, the cording should be cut and started again on the other side. It should not be run through, over, or under another line of cording since this can cause the work to pucker.

# ORNAMENT OR PINCUSHION    Difficulty Level: Easy

Please see Quilting in the chapter on Basic Techniques before beginning.

This project and the one which follows it provides a sample of each kind of trapunto—stuffed trapunto and cording. The ornament is easy to do and takes little time. The only special tools you'll need are a tapestry needle and a stuffing tool.

## MATERIALS

8″ square of gold satin
8″ square of loosely woven muslin
8″ square of red satin
Gold thread
Yarn for cording

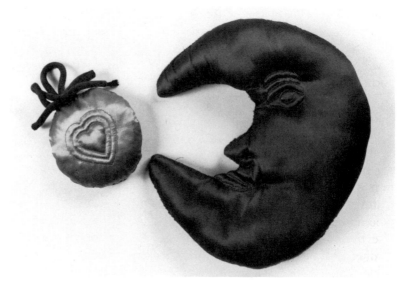

*Fig. 12-6. Ornament (left) and Moon Pillow (right) projects.*

## TEMPLATE DIAGRAM

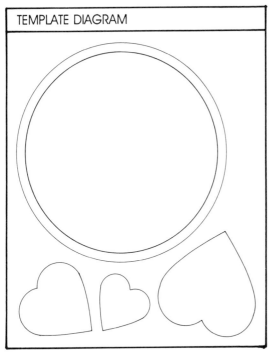

*Templates for this project look like this and are found at the back of the book.*

Few handfuls of polyester stuffing
Red ribbon or braid

## DIRECTIONS

1. Trace the double circle pattern onto tracing paper. The double outline of this pattern will enable you to make two templates—one larger one for the cutting line of pieces, one smaller one for the sewing line. Use the tracing paper circles to make two cardboard circle templates. Use the larger circle to mark a cutting line on the top fabric, muslin backing, and project back. Use the inner circle to mark a sewing line on each of these. Then cut out each one.

2. Trace the three heart cutouts to make cardboard templates as previously done with the circles.

3. Baste the top fabric circle (right side up) to the muslin backing with its marked side out. Use large basting stitches all the way around the outside edge.

4. Center the smallest heart in the middle of the large fabric circle right side up. Trace around the heart using a chalk pencil. Do the same for the next two larger hearts to produce one small heart drawn within two larger ones. The center heart will be stuffed trapunto style. The two larger, surrounding hearts will be corded.

5. Working with the marked heart circle facing up, use a back stitch to quilt along each of the marked heart outlines, one at a time. Quilt each heart. Finish off by knotting the thread and go on to the next heart without crossing over into another heart. Be sure each stitch goes through both layers of fabric. Keep the thread pulled taut, but not so tight that the fabric puckers. Use a length of thread two feet or less to discourage tangling. If you have problems with thread becoming knotted, run it through a cake of beeswax before sewing.

6. When all the heart outlines have been

stitched, begin cording the outermost heart first. Thread a blunt tapestry needle with yarn. Do not knot the end. Working with the piece muslin side up, insert the needle into the outer heart passageway. Pull the thread through the passageway as far as it will comfortably go. Bring the needle out through the backing fabric of the passageway. Then reinsert the needle through the hole out of which it came. Leave about a ½″ extra yarn pulled out as you finish cording the outer heart. Then go on to the middle one, leaving the inside heart untouched.

7. Stuff the inner heart by cutting a tiny hole in the backing or opening the threads in one spot with a tool. Stuff, then sew the hole closed or re-close the threads of the backing fabric by working at them with your tool.

8. When all of the stuffing is completed, take the cut and marked project back and pin the stuffed circle or project front to the project back with right sides together. If you are making an ornament, mark where you want the top of your hanging ornament to be. A loop of ribbon will go here for hanging so the trapunto heart will be right side up when the project is done. Leaving the top part of the circle unsewn for about 2″, sew around the outside of the circle to join front and back parts.

9. Turn the trapunto piece right side out and stuff with polyester filling. Pin the loop of ribbon in place for hanging if you are making an ornament. Sew the last of the circle closed.

# MAN IN THE MOON PILLOW   Difficulty Level: Easy to Moderate

Please see Quilting in the chapter on Basic Techniques before beginning and Fig. 12-6.

This project uses only the stuffing technique and, being larger, requires a little more time than the ornament. A suitable tool for working in the stuffing is required.

## MATERIALS

14″ square red satin
14″ square dark blue velvet
Red quilting thread
Small bag polyester stuffing

## DIRECTIONS

1. Trace the three pieces of the basic moon pattern (without drawing the face) onto tracing paper. The double outer line of this template will enable you to make two templates, one larger one for the cutting line of fabric pieces and one smaller one for the sewing line. Tape the three pieces of the

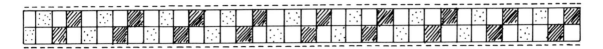

## TEMPLATE DIAGRAM

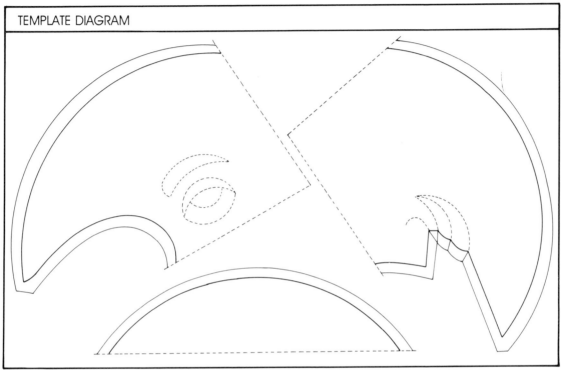

*Templates for this project look like this and are found at the back of the book.*

moon together. Use this to make the two full size moon-shaped cardboard templates. Use the outer moon outline to mark a cutting line on top fabric, muslin backing, and pillow back. Use the inner moon line to mark a sewing line on each of these. Then cut out each one.

2. Baste the top fabric, with right side up, to the muslin backing with marked side out. Use large basting stitches all around the outside edge.

3. Refer back to the moon face drawn on half of the moon pattern. Use it as a general guide in drawing a face of your own on the right side of the top fabric with a chalk pencil.

4. Working with the chalked-in moon face facing up, use a back stitch to quilt along each of the marked moon features: eyebrow, eyelid, eye, pupil, curve of the nostril, and lips. Stitch each without crossing over into another feature. Be sure each

Italy: Trapunto   **145**

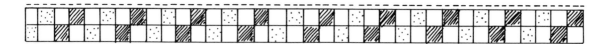

stitch goes through both layers of fabric. Keep the thread pulled gently taut, but not so tight that the fabric puckers. Knot the thread as you finish. Use a length of thread no more than 2' long to discourage tangling. If tangling becomes a problem, run the thread over a cake of beeswax before sewing.

5. When all of the features have been sewn, open a little hole in each one and stuff in the polyester stuffing. To make a hole for the stuffing, make a slit with scissors or open the backing threads with a tool. When done stuffing each feature, sew the slit closed or work the threads shut again with the tool.

6. When all of the stuffing is completed, take the cut and marked pillow back. With right sides together, pin the two—the moon face (or project front) and the pillow back. Sew the front and back together using the marked sewing line as a guide. Leave about three inches unsewn to allow for turning the project right side out.

7. Once the pillow is turned right side out, use the remaining stuffing to fill out the main part of the pillow. You may want to use scissor points to help get the stuffing into the points of the half moon. When the pillow is stuffed full, pin the opening shut and sew closed.

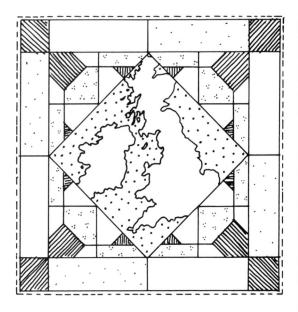

# Chapter Thirteen

English Method Piecing

# A BRIEF HISTORY OF QUILTING IN ENGLAND

London, with all its modern activity, is still a city where age-old rituals survive. You may watch the Ceremony of the Keys at the Tower of London, the changing of the guard in front of Buckingham Palace, heckle the soapbox orators at Speaker's Corner in Hyde Park, or perhaps even happen upon an errant team of Morris dancers in ribbons and bells entertaining the city dwellers. One can visit the incomparable Victoria and Albert Museum. With its 70,000 piece collection of textiles and costumes, it is a treat for any quilter. Here too needleworkers can visit the British Museum and see what is believed to be the earliest example of quilting wrought in stone in the form of an Egyptian pharoah's statue.

At its height, the Roman Empire extended far to the west to encompass England. (Thanks to durable Roman roads, some of which can still be seen in England today, travelers between Rome and London moved with greater ease in the first century A.D. than at the start of the 19th century.[1]) Did the ancient Romans or the Britons whom they struggled to subjugate know of quilting or patchwork? At this time, we do not know. Some Roman and Roman-influenced sculpture from this period has decorative carving that suggests the same kind of texture produced by lines of quilting. Textiles that survive from the pe-riod feature mostly woven decorative elements, but research may one day bring quilted or patchwork examples to light.

The Romans probably slept on quilted bedding—the precursor of our own modern quilts. Our English word "quilt" has as its Latin antecedent, the word *culcitra*. In addition, the ancient Romans enjoyed the beauty and precision of patterns such as those we reproduce in patterns like Flying Geese, Tumbling Blocks, and Variable Star (Fig. 13-1). They used combinations of triangles, squares, and rectangles, familiar to any modern quilter, in their tiled walls and floors seen in many English towns to this day.[2] (For more information on where to find Roman mosaics in Great Britain, see Robert

*Fig. 13-1. Tumbling blocks design done in English piecing, c.1890. From the Stamford Historical Society collection.*

Field's book *Geometric Patterns from Roman Mosaics* listed in the Recommended Reading.)

If quilting and patchwork were known to these ancients and then forgotten during the Dark Ages, it would hardly come as a surprise. Learning stagnated in those grim times. Europe only regained the lost learning of the ancient Romans and Greeks by coming into contact with the Arabic world which had preserved it.

By 720, the Saracens had captured most of Spain and before much longer were ruling Sicily. By the end of the 11th century, the reconquest of Spain and Sicily from the Arabs, the opening of trade routes to the Middle East, and the Crusades all provided a means for Europeans to be touched by the surviving knowledge of the ancient world. But this took time in an age in which the average daily journey was seven miles (the distance a rider could go and return before sundown[3]). Still, that contact sparked the development of civilization revitalizing philosophy, astronomy, mathematics, law, religion, and the arts.

Quilting books traditionally credit the Crusades as the single major event that brought quilting to the European world. Until more is known about the origins of quiltmaking, though, we cannot say for sure that this is what actually took place. It is even possible the Europeans did not discover quilting in the Middle East as much as they rediscovered it. In any case, the First Crusade took place in 1095 with British knights participating. Those that returned home brought with them a grim new knowledge of war. "The flank attack, the concealment of troops, the feigned retreat . . . lighter armor and weapons . . ."[4] were among the innovations gleaned from the East.

If western contact with the Arabic world is indeed how quilting arrived in Europe, then it is ironic that the gentle art of quilting has descended to us through the "arts" of war, for quilting is what distinguished the "lighter armor" of the Saracens. Wearing lightweight, tough quilted jackets topped by chain mail, the Arabs routed the heavily armored Europeans. In view of this, it is perhaps not surprising that quilted clothing gained popularity in Europe during the Middle Ages.

Appliqué was also used during the Middle Ages to decorate heraldic banners and as an inexpensive alternative to richly woven tapestries. Embroidery was extremely popular in its own right and surviving appliquéd pieces are often supplemented with embroidered decoration. A 15th century appliquéd hanging portraying the Tristram legend may be found in the Victoria and Albert Museum. In it, men, women, horses and other design motifs are appliquéd and outlined with cording.

Of the quilts made in England during this period, none survive. We can guess that they existed from historical records of the times. Inventories of household goods were kept during the Middle Ages to determine property taxes. A "quylt," "qwilt," or "twylt" appeared in various records to mean a quilted bed covering.

Quilts were also mentioned in lyric poems of the time. In *Sir Gawain and the Green Knight*, the hero is treated as an honored guest: "A chair before the chimney where charcoal was burning/ was made ready in his room, all arrayed and covered/ with cushions upon quilted cloths that were cunningly made."[5]

Context is important in old references such as these since words similar to "quilt" were sometimes used to describe a stuffed mattress on which to sleep rather than a quilted coverlet.[6] Whether the kinds of quilts cited in literary references were made routinely in England, we can only guess. Given that the poems are themselves works of fiction, they might have even referred to quilts imported from the East as easily as to those made at home.

In medieval England, quilted "jacks" or jackets for men offered protection from the cold as well as the thrust of a dagger. Quilting was also used for sleepwear in the 1500s, especially night shirts and sleeping caps.

Quilted clothes remained popular for fashionable Britons of the 17th and 18th centuries. Quilted jackets were of less defensive use after the introduction of firearms, but were no less popular as stylish clothing. Quilted garments included waistcoats for men, as well as dresses and petticoats for women. In addition, quilted bed coverings and hangings kept off draughts and offered privacy.

The earliest known surviving English patchwork, the Levens Hall quilt, was made in 1708. About this time, quilts began to be available to other than strictly wealthy families as can be seen from inventories of furnishings made upon the death of a householder. Central Medallion quilts were popular, and many were done in Broderie Persé technique (about which more will be discussed in Chapter Fourteen). Also popular was the all-over pieced Honeycomb design (what we call Grandmother's Flower Garden). This pattern was typically executed in the paper template method. In this technique, paper templates were sewn behind each bit of fabric to stiffen and secure it. The result was beautifully precise patchwork.

Modern historians are especially excited to find a quilt top made in the paper template method, what we would call English piecing. Such heirlooms, complete with templates cut from discarded letters, pages from antique copy books, or old handwritten receipts, tell a great deal about the work, its maker, and dates of construction.

Years ago, paper was a scarcer commodity than it is today. Even scraps were hoarded thriftily, which explains why so many older unfinished quilt tops made in this method have templates in which writing appears. It would have been unthinkable to use a fresh sheet of paper when a used one would answer just as well. In our own time of recycling woes, we can take a lesson from our forebears about making every useful bit of paper count.

As the Industrial Revolution gained momentum, British-made cotton fabrics became more widely available at reasonable prices. With the arrival of the 19th century, quilting became less a pastime of ladies of leisure and established itself as a rural British tradition.[7]

As quilters, we can all draw inspiration from Elizabeth Fry, a 19th century British quiltmaker. This patient Quaker reformer used patchwork as a vehicle for bettering the conditions of women prisoners in her time. Conditions in 19th century prisons were appalling. Stephen Grellet, a Quaker and former French aristocrat, was inspired to write of the squalor of the women's quarters at Newgate: ". . . the foulness of the air was almost insupportable. . . ." In the infirmary, he "found many very sick, lying on the bare floor or on some old straw, having very scanty covering over them, though it was quite cold; and there were several children born in the prison among them, almost naked."[8]

Upon hearing of the problem, Elizabeth Fry organized other women members of the Society of Friends. In time, she and her followers set up sewing classes for the inmates who were taught to make clothes and do patchwork from donated scraps. It was not easy work; she had to contend not only with indifferent bureaucrats, but with the prevalent idea that the poor were meant to be so. Elizabeth Fry did even more; she provided patchwork scraps and other comforts, such as tea, to women condemned to be transported to penal colonies. The making of a quilt during the long voyage provided such women, many of whom were penniless, with a marketable item on their arrival.

During the 19th century, English quilts continued to be made mostly in medallion and all-over patterns. The same period saw a rise in America of countless block patterns. In the late 1880s, English needleworkers were inspired by the crazy quilt mania that had swept America a few years earlier. The passion for crazy quilts in England, as in America, was eventually supplanted by renewed interest in traditional patchwork which has remained viable to this day.

## NOTES

1. Roger Butterfield, *Ancient Rome* (New York: Odyssey Press, 1964), p. 31.

2. For a discussion of an additional connection between English quilting and the ancient Romans, see *The Quilts of the British Isles* by Janet Rae (New York: Dutton, 1987, p. 68) in which she connects the Log Cabin pattern with the way in which farmland was divided in Roman times in Great Britain. In "run-rig" or strip farming, narrow bands of wet, cultivated land and dry, fallow land were "laid out in parallel strips which run at right angles to each

other", like the positioning of dark (corresponding to wet land) and light (corresponding to dry land) fabric strips in the Log Cabin pattern. Her observations suggest that the Log Cabin pattern may have very old antecedents.

3. James Burke, *The Day the Universe Changed*, Boston: Little, Brown & Co., 1985, p. 92.

4. Harold Lamb, *The Crusades*, Garden City, NY: Garden City Publishing Company, 1930.

5. *Sir Gawain and the Green Knight, Pearl, and Sir Orfeo*, trans. by J.R.R. Tolkien (Boston: Houghton Mifflin Co., 1975), p. 47.

6. Averil Colby, *Quilting* (London: B.T. Batsford, 1972), p. 99.

7. Dorothy Osler, *Traditional British Quilts* (London: B.T. Batsford, 1987), p. 95.

8. Walter Russell Bowie, *Women of Light* (New York: Harper & Row, 1963), p. 64.

# TECHNIQUES OF ENGLISH PIECING

English patchwork has long made use of its own distinctive sewing method. Traditionally, English quilts were made of hexagons, diamonds, or triangles and were done in the "paper template" technique often called "English" piecing (Fig. 13-2). In this method, the fabric is wrapped around a piece of regular paper cut to shape and basted securely to it. Then the basted fabric/template pieces are joined together by being whip-stitched at the edges. The whole project is ironed from the back with the templates in place. Then the basting stitches are taken out and the templates usually removed. (In some quilts, especially silk ones meant to be left unquilted, the templates are left in.)

"American" style piecing, on the other hand, uses running stitches and cardboard

*Fig. 13-2. Antique hexagon pattern (unfinished) in English piecing with handwritten letters used as templates still in place.*

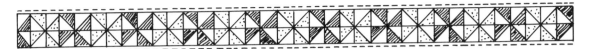

templates (not paper ones) to mark fabric only. By comparison, the English method at first glance appears more fussy, the American one certainly faster and, for that reason, perhaps more practical. The English method, however, is also more precise. It is easier in a sense for a beginner to use since, although more time-consuming, it achieves perfect piecing every time. In English piecing, the edges are always sharp and crisp, the seams always straight.

Just when is it best to use English piecing? When a design incorporates oddly juxtaposed angles, the slight stiffness provided to the entire project by the paper template method is helpful. It gives the work support as it is being sewn and makes sewing easier. Also, if one is at all insecure about creating perfectly straight and crisp seams, the English method offers consistently fool-proof results. It is more time-consuming, but for a person who spends any time ripping out and re-sewing pieced shapes, English piecing may not be that much more lengthy in the long run.

English piecing is especially appropriate for producing intricate geometric designs. One appealing source for such designs can be found in the Roman artifacts that remain in Great Britain today. As discussed earlier in this chapter, the Romans brought with them the craft of making exquisite mosaics, many of which may be found today in different parts of England. In what is now Silchester, there once flourished the Romano-British town of

Calleva Atrebatum. A mosaic-tiled floor from a house that stood there serves as the basis for one of the projects included here. Preserved today at the Reading Museum in Reading, Berkshire, it features a number of appealing patterns that lend themselves to English piecing (Fig. 13-3).

The second project offered here appropriately makes use of another form of British "tiling." Mathematicians delight in devising tilings or tesselations—ways of covering a plane with congruent polygons. The Dutch artist M.C. Escher is famous for his tesselations using interlocking shapes that suggest animals and other forms. British mathematical physicist Dr. Roger Penrose

*Fig. 13-3. Sketch of tile from a Romano-British mosaic floor from Silchester, England.*

discovered two shapes which he calls "a dart" and "a kite." These can be joined in a variety of interlocking ways to create a kaleidoscope-like symmetrical image which radiates to infinity, if you care to take it that far.

Kaleidoscope-style wall hangings have been popularized in recent years by a number of contemporary quilters. You may have seen the intricate, colorful "mandalas" of quilt artist Katie Pasquini. The complex symmetry of kaleidoscopic quilts makes them ideal for English method piecing.

They are, nonetheless, extremely challenging to produce. This difficulty can be greatly reduced with the help of Dr. Penrose's tiles. Astonishing variety can be achieved through the manipualtion of only two basic shapes. Moreover, if you have any mathematicians in the family, they'll be much impressed with your use of Penrose tiles. (If you really want to impress them, take a look at Martin Gardner's article "Mathematical Games" from the January 1977 issue of *Scientific American*, pages 110–121 for a little background information.)

# HERB PILLOW

## Difficulty Level: Easy

The gift of an herb pillow is a delightful English custom, one that you can enjoy upon finishing this project. The pattern here is based on one of the mosaics in the Romano-British floor at Silchester discussed earlier. This same floor contains many different designs based on four- and five-

*Fig. 13-4. English Herb Pillow project.*

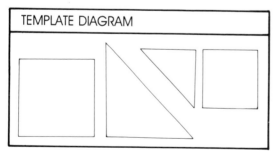

TEMPLATE DIAGRAM

*Templates for this project look like this and are found at the back of the book.*

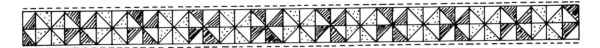

square blocks, any one of which is a good starting point for trying the English method of piecing.

## MATERIALS

¼ yard yellow calico
¼ yard yellow, red and blue (multi-colored) calico
¼ yard solid yellow fabric
8½″ square cut from one of the above fabrics for pillow backing
Bond paper for templates
Several handfuls polyester stuffing
Two cupfuls scented dried herbs and flowers

## DIRECTIONS

1. In American-style piecing, you use one template for each shape. In this English piecing project you will be using two templates for each shape. The large template is for cutting the fabric shapes with seam allowance included. The small template is for the paper shapes around which the fabric shapes are basted. Be clear on which is large and which is small before you start marking or cutting fabric.

2. Use the large templates to mark and cut fabric shapes. To follow the sample project exactly, you will need 12 yellow calico squares, 5 multi-colored squares, 4 multi-colored triangles, 4 solid yellow squares, and 4 solid yellow triangles. See Fig. 13-4 for placement.

3. Use the small templates to cut paper shapes for basting fabric shapes. Use regular bond or any other paper that will hold its shape as you sew around it. Don't use paper, however, that is so heavy you will have difficulty pushing the needle through it. You will need 21 paper squares and 8 paper triangles.

4. Place all of the fabric shapes wrong side up on your work surface. Center a paper template directly in the middle of each fabric shape and pin in place.

5. Baste the fabric shapes around each paper template. The shapes may be sewn in any order. To begin, take a shape and hold it so the pinned paper (and wrong side of the fabric shape) is facing you. Fold one seam allowance over the paper. Do not fold the paper, however. Let its edge be your folding guide. In the middle of the folded-over seam allowance, take a basting stitch. Go through both the paper and the fabric. Use a contrasting color of basting thread to make removal of the basting easier later. Going around the shape, fold over the next seam allowance and baste with a single stitch. Continue this way all around the shape until you reach the last seam allowance. Do not make a knot. Cut the thread leaving about an inch extra, remove the pin and set aside. Baste all the remaining shapes in the same way.

6. Iron all of the basted shapes.

7. Beginning with the top row, join the shapes. Start with the two left-hand triangles. Place them right sides together and match the corners. Use a whipstitch to join them along the long side. Do not run the thread through the paper. Your stitching should be dense. Traditionally, women took as many as fifteen to twenty tiny whipstitches to the inch. Use your judgement as to how dense to make your stitching, but the more stitches, the neater your work will appear when finished. Be sure to knot your thread before starting and take one or two backstitches at the end. Join all of the shapes to form the design, row by row. Then join the rows.

8. When all of the shapes have been joined, pull out the basting threads and lift out the papers. The papers may be saved and used again on another project. Iron the sewn herb pillow top.

9. With right sides together, center the herb pillow top on the 8½″ square pillow back. Pin in place and trim excess pillow backing if necessary. Sew the herb pillow front to the back on three sides, leaving one side open to stuff with polyester filling and scented dried herbs and flowers. Turn the pillow right side out and stuff, then sew the remaining side closed to complete the project.

# KALEIDOSCOPE WALL HANGING    Difficulty Level: Moderate to Challenging

With the help of tilings designed by reknowned British mathematician Roger Penrose, almost anyone can create a complex-looking kaleidoscopic image in English piecing method. It is strongly recommended, however, that you complete the English Herb Pillow project before starting this more difficult project. Remember, there are two templates for each shape, one large and one small. The large ones are for cutting out fabric shapes; the small for cutting paper templates around which fabric shapes are basted. See completed project in the color section (Plate 14).

## MATERIALS

One 4″ × 36″ strip blue solid
One 4″ × 36″ strip blue calico
½ yard each: magenta calico, black and blue solid
¼ yard each (9″ × 45″): blue calico, magenta solid, teal, purple, and green
Three 2″ × 45″ black strips for binding
36″ × 36″ square batting
36″ × 36″ backing fabric
Bond paper for paper templates
Navy quilting thread
Black thread for joining fabric templates

*Fig. 13-5. Kaleidoscope Wall Hanging project.*

## DIRECTIONS

1. You will be working with only two basic shapes, the "kite" and the "dart." Trace the large kite and large dart onto cardboard and cut out for templates. Cut the shapes so that they are facing up and down on the fabric grain. Use the templates to mark and cut darts in the following colors:

Blue solid: 10 darts, 10 kites
Blue calico: 5 darts

Magenta solid: 10 kites
Magenta calico: 5 kites, 10 darts
Black: 10 kites, 5 darts
Teal: 10 kites
Purple: 10 kites
Green: 10 darts

2. Sew the two 4″ × 36″ blue calico and blue solid strips together down one long side with a ⅜″ seam allowance. Place the large kite template on this combined strip so that the seam between the two colors runs

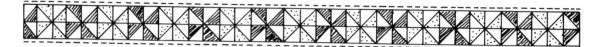

## TEMPLATE DIAGRAM

*Templates for this project look like this and are found at the back of the book.*

right down the middle of the kite. Cut out five 2-color kites.

3. Use the small templates to cut paper shapes for basting the fabric shapes. You will need 60 kites and 40 darts. The quickest way to proceed is to photocopy several copies of the small kites and darts, group them on a single page and photocopy the page.

4. Place all of the fabric kites wrong side up on your work surface. Center a smaller paper kite directly in the middle of each and pin in place. Do the same for all of the fabric darts. When pinning the five 2-color kites for the center of the kaleidoscope, be especially careful that the seam between the two colors runs down the exact center of the paper template.

5. Baste the fabric shapes around each paper template. Use a contrasting color of basting thread for ease in removing later. As you finish basting each shape, do not knot the thread, but cut it off with about an inch to spare. Remove the pin and set aside.

6. Iron all of the basted fabric shapes.

7. To join the shapes, start from the center of the kaleidoscope and work outward. Follow the piecing diagram (Fig. 13-6 and see Plate 14). Use a whipstitch to join the shapes along one side at a time. Run the thread just through the edge of each fabric shape, not through the paper. When the center circular pattern is sewn, begin adding on the next ring of shapes. Continue in this way until all of the shapes are joined.

8. When all of the shapes have been sewn together, pull out the basting threads and lift out the papers. Iron the kaleidoscope project top.

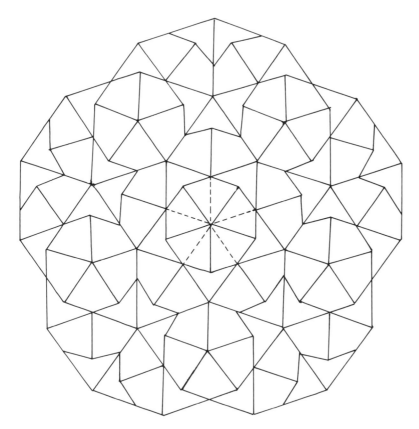

*Fig. 13-6. Kaleidoscope Wall Hanging piecing diagram.*

9. Place the wall hanging backing on your work surface right side down. Lay the batting over this. Lay the kaleidoscope project top right side up on top of these. Pin and baste in place. Then trim the excess batting and backing to within 2″ of the top all the way around.

10. Quilt the project, running lines of quilting ¼″ inside each shape. Or tack the project, using black thread and putting in a single tack at each corner where two fabric shapes meet. Pull all tacking threads to the back and lose them in the batting.

11. Trim the excess 2″ of the batting and backing fabric from around the outside of the project. Bind the outer edges, using the black binding strips to complete the project.

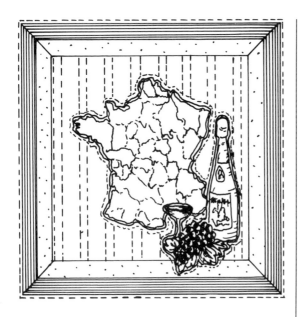

# Chapter 14

# France: Broderie Perse

# QUILTS: OBJETS D'ART

The contrast between old and new in Paris is almost startling. Modern buildings with sharp gray edges point to the future, while Notre Dame, the Sorbonne, and the Place de la Concorde all hint at the past. The present is also very much alive in a city where you can watch people pass by your nook in a cafe, browse the book stalls along the Seine, or wander tree-lined boulevards.

Like a receding tide casting its treasures on the shore, the international exposition of 1889 left behind it the symbol of the city—La Tour Eiffel. Soundly despised in its early days, the tower has endured and it is a rare tourist who does not view the panoramic scene from its heights.

As lovers of artwork and old textiles, quilters can find much to enjoy in Paris. One can visit the artists who still haunt Montmartre, explore the Cluny Museum with its famous unicorn tapestries, or hunt antique sewing tools in the Sunday flea markets at the edge of the city.

France has always had a strong needlework and textile tradition. In medieval castles, ladies tended to their household responsibilities which included spinning, weaving, and needlework. As they sat and worked, they sometimes sang "chansons de toile" or sewing songs of which *Fair Yolande* was one:

*Fair Yolande in a chamber still,*
*On her knee some stuffs unfolds,*
*Sews with a thread of gold and one of silk.*
*Her stern mother chides her;*
*"I chide you for it, Fair Yolande."*

*"Fair Yolande, I chide you,*
*You are my daughter, do your duty."*
*"My lady mother, what is it for?"*
*"I chide you for it, Fair Yolande."*

*"Mother, for what do you chide me?*
*Is it for sewing or cutting,*
*Or spinning or brushing,*
*Or is it for sleeping too much?"*
*"I chide you for it, Fair Yolande."*

*"It is not for sewing nor for cutting,*
*Nor for spinning nor for brushing;*
*Nor is it for too much sleeping,*
*But for speaking too much to the knight.*
*I chide you for it, Fair Yolande."*[1]

The bed and its accoutrements were of considerable importance in the Middle Ages in France as in other parts of Europe. The practice of donating such possessions upon one's death to a hospital or convent suggests the value that was attached to these furnishings. In her will dated 1262, for instance, Agnes de Faucigny stipulated that her feather bed and its coverlets be given to the convent where she was raised.[2]

By the 1500s and 1600s, intarsia embroidery, a form of appliqué, was being produced in all of the countries of Europe, including France. Fancy needlework was a

pastime of the queens and noblewomen of Renaissance France. Mary Queen of Scots learned her needlework skills as a young girl at the French Court. They were skills which would stand her in good stead years later during her long imprisonment in England where her work can still be seen at Hardwick Hall.

In the 1600s, the establishment of the British East India Company brought large numbers of Eastern textiles onto the European market. The technique of broderie perse, whose name comes from the French for "persian embroidery," made use of these Indian hand-printed and painted cottons. Broderie perse became popular in France, England, and later in America as well.

Indian cottons or "chintz" were greatly admired by Europeans who had no comparable fabrics nor indeed the know-how to manufacture them at the time. Chintz, whose name was derived from a Hindi word "chint," meaning "variegated in color," was being made as early as 400 B.C. in the East. Its colors and designs seemed wildly exotic to western eyes.

Broderie perse was the art of cutting out the printed chintz fabric motifs, turning them under at the edges and appliquéing them to a solid color background in a rearranged design. In France and England, it was feared the home textile industries would not prove equal to the challenge presented by the colorful Indian cottons. In both countries serious efforts were made to suppress the imports.[3] Nonetheless, many

of the foreign textiles made their way into European ports. Quilters seized upon them eagerly. Cutting out the individual floral or figural motifs and appliquéing them to new (usually white) backgrounds, they made the most of lengths of fabric too small, perhaps, for an entire bed covering and in the process created their own unique designs.

Indian palampores, large block-printed cotton panels, were produced to order in India for the European market. Originally their designs had been inspired by early Persian manuscripts, but they eventually came to incorporate motifs from Hindu, Islamic, Chinese, and even European sources.[4] The central flowering tree-of-life design was especially popular for use in broderie perse. With its gently twining branches surrounded by a border of vines and florals, it was characterized by brilliant colors and finely wrought designs. Additional bold, cheerful motifs included animated human figures, birds, and animals.

The broderie perse technique of cutting out printed fabric pictures had several advantages. It made the most of a small piece of fabric. In addition, the white background had the effect of throwing the appliquéd forms into high relief, creating a resemblance to more time-consuming embroidery which was itself very popular during the period. It has even been romantically surmised that the broderie perse technique may have helped to protect some of the sailors and sea captains who brought the prohibited fabrics home to their wives. It was illegal to import the large, uncut

Fig. 14-1. Broderie Perse quilt, c.1840, from Montgomery County, Maryland. Photograph courtesy of The Baltimore Museum of Art, Maryland. Gift of Dr. and Mrs. M. Lee Williams.

*Fig. 14-2. "Flowers and Birds" child's quilt, c.1825. Photograph courtesy of The Baltimore Museum of Art, Maryland. Gift of Irwin and Linda Berman, St. Simons Island, Georgia.*

palampores, but once these were cut apart and sewn into a new article such as a coverlet, they were no longer quite so incriminating.

By the end of the 1700s, English and French manufacturers were producing large amounts of their own floral-printed chintzes for dress and furnishings. Broderie perse was still considered fashionable in Europe. Although it began to be supplanted by other patchwork styles there, the broderie perse technique traveled on to American shores where it continued to inspire needleworkers well into the nineteenth century.[5]

## NOTES

1. Dorothy Mills, *The Middle Ages* (New York: G.P. Putnam's Sons, 1935), p. 151.

2. Rebecca Martin, *Textiles in Daily Life in the Middle Ages* (Cleveland, OH: Cleveland Museum of Art, 1985), p. 43.

3. Jonathan Holstein, *American Pieced Quilts* (New York: Viking Press, 1972), p. 9.

4. Dilys Blum and Jack L. Lindsey, "Nineteenth-Century Appliqué Quilts," *The Bulletin* (Philadelphia Museum of Art, vol. 85, Fall 1989), p. 12.

5. Jonathan Holstein, *The Pieced Quilt: An American Tradition* (Boston: Little, Brown, and Company, 1973), p. 21.

# TECHNIQUES OF BRODERIE PERSE

Selecting an appropriate appliqué fabric is the first step in this technique. Choose a fabric with prints that are finely detailed, yet large enough to sew with ease. Tightly woven and/or polished cottons resist fraying.

If your new, planned background is light, avoid chintz cut outs that have been printed on a dark ground. Likewise, if your planned background is dark, avoid prints with a light ground. Otherwise, you will have to be very meticulous is turning under the cut outs to avoid an unpleasant shadow effect should a bit of the old background show.

In picture quilts, broderie perse cut outs can be combined with regular appliqués to give a hint of three-dimensionality to the design. Use detailed broderie perse appliqués to the front and regular appliqués to the back to suggest distance.

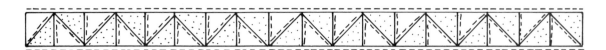

*Fig. 14-3. "South Hill," by author, 1987. Contemporary adaptation of broderie perse technique using printed fabric cutouts and solid color fabric appliqués.*

# ZEPHYR'S WINDOW

Please see Appliqué and Quilting in the chapter on Basic Techniques and Fig. 14-4 before beginning.

In this project, the technique of broderie perse is expanded upon to provide a challenge for contemporary quiltmakers comfortable with pictorial appliqué. In choosing fabrics, be sure the patterned appliqués contrast well with the floral chintzes used in the flowerpot and outside the window.

## Difficulty Level: Moderate to Challenging

### SUGGESTED VARIATIONS

You may want to try painting your own flower or cat broderie perse appliqués instead of buying printed fabrics.

### MATERIALS

18″ × 18″ square unbleached muslin
1 fat quarter of each: light green solid (window); mustard yellow solid (daylight);

*Fig. 14-4. Zephyr's Window project.*

maroon solid (flowerpot); patterned brown fabric (cat)

1 large pictorial chintz appliqué (flowers in pot)

3 small chintz appliqués (flowers outside window)

4″ × 12″ strip patterned blue fabric (tablecloth)

Four 4″ × 22″ strips maroon calico (borders)

Four 2″ × 27″ strips blue (binding)

28 × 28″ square backing fabric

30 × 30″ square batting

## DIRECTIONS

1. To make templates, trace the patterns for the window, yellow "daylight" rectangles, flowerpot, and cat.

2. To make the window frame, fold a rectangle of light green fabric in fourths. Place the template on the fabric to correspond with folded and non-folded fabric sides as shown in template. Mark and cut out the window.

## TEMPLATE DIAGRAM

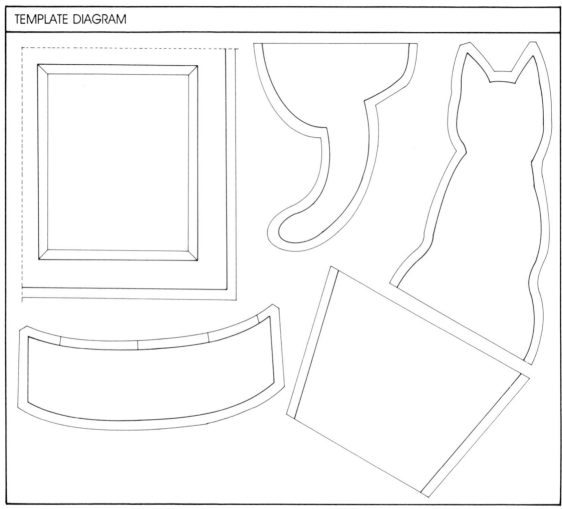

*Templates for this project look like this and are found at the back of the book.*

3. Using the window pane template, mark and cut out the daylight rectangles. Also mark and cut the two flowerpot pieces and the cat.

4. Carefully cut out the appliqués you have chosen. Cut so as to leave a ¼″ margin all the way around the appliqué. Clip any curves that turn in. (Outward turning curves need

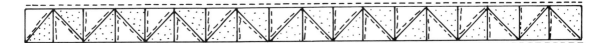

not be clipped.) The large appliqué will slightly overlap the top part of the flowerpot. The three small appliqués will appear "through" the window.

5. Lay out all of the cut out pieces of the pattern in the position in which they are to be sewn. To position your appliqués accurately, you may find it easier to baste under the edges first rather than pinning the appliqués in place and turning them under as you sew. To begin sewing, turn under the bottom and left side of the window. Leave the top and right window fabric edges raw. Turn under all of the inside window edges except those at the bottom of the window. Turn this edge under and pin it rather than sew it. (Leave these edges unsewn as they will cover the raw stem edges of the three small flower appliqués.) Position the yellow "daylight" rectangles so their raw edges are covered by the turned under inner window edges. Pin in place on the muslin background and appliqué with matching thread.

6. Turn under the fabric appliqués for the flowerpot and cat. The flowerpot is in two pieces. For the bottom part of the flowerpot, turn under only the sides. The raw edges at top and bottom of this piece will be covered by other parts of the design.

7. Turn under one long edge of the blue tablecloth on which the cat sits.

8. Position and pin the flowerpot, table-cloth, and cat. Sew in place using matching thread.

9. Using thread that matches as closely as possible (given that the cut outs are multi-colored), turn under the chintz appliqués, taking care to keep the outlines of the leaves and flowers intact. Position the large chintz cut out over the flowerpot top. Turn under any stem edges as needed, or let the flowers and leaves drape over the edge of the flowerpot top if your appliqué is suited to this. Sew in place. Position the small appliqués so that their stem ends are covered by the window frame edge. Sew them in place and then sew the window frame.

10. With right sides together, join each of the border strips to the appliquéd top (Fig. 14-5). Then join the leftover strip edges to complete the border.

11. If you like, stuff the large chintz appliqué to give it a close-up "realistic" look and add perspective to the design. To do this, sew a fairly close running stitch around each individual leaf and flower. Using a pair of iris scissors or a needlework awl, open up the background fabric behind each sewn flower or leaf. Stuff a little extra polyester filling into each motif until it is well filled. Then close over the hole in the backing with loose stitching.

12. To prepare the project for quilting, place the backing fabric right side down,

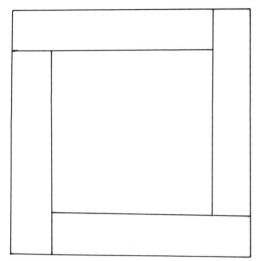

*Fig. 14-5. Diagram for joining borders.*

then the batting, and place the appliquéd top fabric on all of these right side up. Pin and baste.

13. Quilt the project. Quilt ¼" around the outside of each appliquéd motif. Use quilter's masking tape to quilt straight diagonal lines in the yellow "daylight" rectangles and the white "wall" spaces, or try another quilting pattern of your own choosing.

14. Remove the basting threads and trim the excess batting and backing fabric.

15. Bind the project using the narrow blue strips. Add loops at the top for hanging if desired.

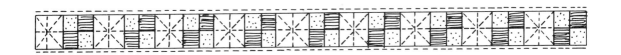

# Part Six: CENTRAL AND SOUTH AMERICA

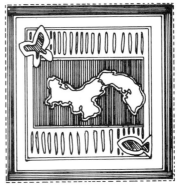

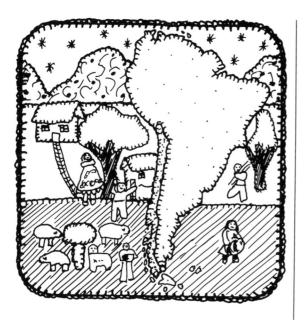

# Chapter Fifteen | Chile: Arpilleras

# ARPILLERAS: A SILENT PROTEST

Bordered by the snow-capped Andes on one side and by 5,000 miles of Pacific ocean on the other, Chile has the longest coastline of any nation in the world. Poet Pablo Neruda has written often of his country, bringing its sunny warmth and natural beauty into the mind's eye of readers around the world:

*In Chile now, cherries are dancing,*
*the dark mysterious girls are singing,*
*and in guitars, water is shining.*
*The sun is touching every door*
*and making wonder of the wheat . . .*[1]

Santiago, the capital, is at the center of this long, narrow country. Here the Andes form a textured backdrop that is gently echoed in the many little hills within the city itself. The Alameda, the main downtown street, runs through Santa Lucia Hill, one of the loveliest parks in the Americas. A short walk across the Mapocho River is San Cristobal Hill, crowned with an impressive statue of the Virgin Mary. There is, however, a side to Santiago that many visitors never see—the side of poverty—of cardboard huts, unemployment, communal soup pots, and abandoned buildings.

Meanwhile, the rest of Santiago is bustling. Shops and markets offer the tourist a wide variety of items. In the marketplace are displayed lush fruits and vegetables as well as handicrafts. Among the handwork are small wooden carvings, colorful weav-ings, vivid embroideries, humble clay pots. If one does not see arpilleras (Chilean appliquéd fabric pictures) displayed here, it is because for some time they have been regarded as politically dangerous. How could a piece of needlework be considered threatening? Under a repressive government, such a thing is possible.

The arpillera is a kind of fabric collage. Generally about 12″ × 18″, it is a small horizontal needlework picture of scenes from everyday life. It is sewn together from colorful appliquéd shapes and often depicts farms, city scenes, and villages. Its most distinctive features are the little three-dimensional dolls and other motifs such as vegetables in a garden. Made of cotton cloth in bright colors, it suggests warmth, vitality, movement, and a quality of innocence (Fig. 15-1).

The materials that form the arpilleras are modest and inexpensive. The appliqués are often bordered in simple stitches—chain stitch, cross stitch and blanket stitch. Personal innovations make each arpillera unique. A woman might cut a lock of her own hair to decorate a figure or snip a piece of fabric from her skirt to get the right color.

Many of the arpilleras feature an appliqué rendering of the Andes Mountains in the background. Towering and ever-present in the lives of generations of Chileans, the Andes are still imposing even in the days of modern transportation. Another frequent

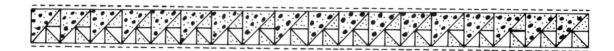

*Fig. 15-1. Chilean arpillera with women tending communal soup pot and Andes mountains in the background.*

motif is a large round sun. To some, it is indicative merely of the warm dry climate of the Andes. To others, it symbolizes warmth and promise. As one maker of arpilleras says, "I put an enormous sun in all my arpilleras, because even though I might not have a cup of tea to my name I never lose my faith."[2]

The craft of arpillera-making is not unique to Chile. Arpilleras are made in Colombia and Peru (Fig. 15-2). Chilean arpilleras, however, have an important difference. For some time now, they have usually been designed to present a strong political message.

In 1973, General Augusto Pinochet came to power in a violent military coup. Over the next decade and a half, thousands of people suspected of opposing his regime were beaten, imprisoned, or executed. Many were dragged from their homes by military police and disappeared never to be heard from again. In December 1989, political moderate Patricio Aylwin won Chile's first presidential election since 1970. His victory signalled the beginning of the end of the authoritarian rule of Pinochet, whose bid to remain in office was rejected in a plebiscite the previous year.

A first glance does not always disclose the political themes of the Chilean arpilleras. In one, for instance, are pictured what look like children in a large dining room and women gathered outdoors around a huge cooking pot. Then we realize we are seeing a church-sponsored child feeding program.

*Fig. 15-2. Peruvian arpillera nativity scene with sheep and houses.*

There is a factory door marked with an X in yarn to symbolize mass unemployment. In reality, the women pictured around the communal soup pot have spent the morning collecting scraps of food from stores, private homes, restaurants, and markets. They gather vegetables of too poor a quality to be sold, the good half of a half-rotten potato or tomato, and make do with what they find.

During the regime of Pinochet, many women lost their husbands and found themselves with no means of financial support.

While some Chilean women held jobs, many more pursued the traditional role of mother and homemaker during the 1970s. As husbands and brothers joined the lists of the Detained and Disappeared, many of these women with families to raise turned in desperation to the church in their communities. With its help, the first arpillera workshops were organized in Santiago.

Arpillera means "burlap" in Spanish. The cloth backing of these small appliquéd and embroidered wall hangings is often of

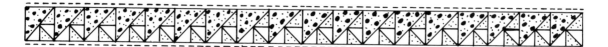

burlap or grain sacks. From this the hangings themselves have come to be called arpilleras. Their makers are the arpilleristas.

At first, the arpilleristas met together to sew their needlework pictures for the sake of emotional support as much as anything. Chilean poet and lecturer on arpilleras Marjorie Agosin has said of the arpilleristas ". . . the arpillera workshop is their life, their daily bread, also a way of feeling accompanied in their sadness. The arpillera is not a creative competition but a way of sharing the preoccupations and worries of their everyday lives."[3]

In time, it became clear that the arpilleras could be sold to help support these women, many of whom were destitute. They were purchased at first by traveling journalists and other tourists and later by consumers outside the country. The Vicarate of Solidarity, an office of the Catholic Archbishop of Santiago, was formed to offer legal aid, health care, and work opportunities to the poor. Only under these auspices could the arpilleristas hope to function in the face of repression. The Vicarate bought the arpilleras from their makers and sold the work abroad, using money from the sales to purchase more arpillera materials.

Perhaps it is the friendly naivete of folk art that makes the arpillera so appealing to many. Yet, if the arpilleras appear childlike, they are anything but childish. They are a small voice amid a storm of protest that has brought about change in a country known for its repressive government. They are proof that even the gentle art of needlework can prove a powerful weapon in the work of freedom (see Plate 16 in the color section).

Many Chileans hope that there will be some form of justice for the Detained and Disappeared. But it is questionable whether the military will be called to account for its role in past political killings. Still, the rejection of authoritarian rule has resulted in some positive change. Even the arpilleras suggest this much. Where a few years ago, their slogans read, "No Mas Tortura" (No More Torture), today they carry a different message "Verdad y Justicia para los Detenidos y Desaparecidos" (Truth and Justice for the Detained and Disappeared). It may be that the hopeful promise of the cheerful appliquéd sun in so many Chilean arpilleras is finally on its way to becoming a reality.

No project has been included for this chapter. Many of the arpilleristas remain impoverished and must rely on their needlework as their only source of income for themselves and their families. Instead of making your own arpillera, you might wish to purchase one directly from the workshops in Santiago. Sending a check for $25 to: Vicaria, Plaza de Armas 444, 20 Piso, Santiago, Chile.

## NOTES

1. Selden Rodman, *South America of the Poets* (New York: Hawthorne Books, 1970), p. 231.

2. Marjorie Agosin, *Scraps of Life: Chilean Arpilleras*, trans. by Cola Franzen (Trenton, NJ: Red Sea Press, 1987), p. 82.

3. Ibid, p. 12.

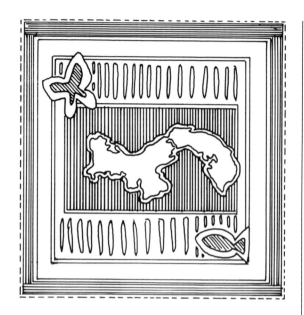

# Chapter Sixteen

# Panama: Mola

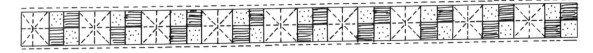

# MOLA MAKING: A WAY OF LIFE

The Comarca de San Blas includes a narrow strip of rain forests along the eastern coast of Panama and its offshore islands. The islands are within easy canoeing distance of the lush, green mainland jungle and the whole is protected by a long barrier reef. It is here that the Cuna Indians, makers of intricately patterned appliqué molas, live and work.

The mola is a colorful cloth panel handstitched in reverse appliqué technique. It is an integral part of a Cuna woman's apparel, just as making molas is part of her daily way of life. Front and back mola panels form the basis of a Cuna woman's blouse. So it is that the word *mola* may refer to the panel from which the blouse is made, or the entire blouse. In our own country, where the Cuna's needlework is often framed and displayed on a wall, the word *mola* usually refers to just the panel.

Devoted to preserving their cultural identity and their equally threatened rain forest, the Cuna Indians have learned, in the words of one American, "to live in contact with the Western world without succumbing to it."[1] That they cannot avoid contact with it is apparent from their needle art. Many molas feature traditional designs of island plants and animals. Colorful portrayals of parrots, pelicans, bats, alligators, lizards, insects, and fish abound. Sometimes the mola makers surprise us, however. They have a way of taking a graphic symbol from a printed American advertisement, complete with English lettering, and transfering it to cloth, giving it unique spirit in the process.

An especially pleasing mola pattern can catch on and be repeated, with personal touches, by other makers. So it is that we have molas featuring the listening dog and gramaphone of the RCA "His Master's Voice" advertisement, as well as recognizable graphic symbols from ads for soap, soft drinks, Singer sewing machines, the Lions Club, and cereal boxes.

The Cunas, however, are determined to allow the acculturation process only so much entry into their lives and no more. Twentieth century life has indeed intruded. In addition to the ads that furnish inspiration for mola designs, there are outboard motors for the dugout canoes used by the islanders, as well as a liberal sprinkling of

*Fig. 16-1. Cuna women selling molas, Panama. Photograph by David M. Schwartz.*

tape decks and boom boxes. More men than in the past leave their families to work in Panama City. The sale of the mola itself has recently superceded that of coconuts as a means of bringing income into this island refuge. But, to a large extent, the Cuna way of life remains the same.

Traditionally the Cunas have guarded their lands from intrusion, maintained their unique cultural identity, and insisted on firm standards of personal behavior. That "grit" or firmness in the face of encroaching civilization has stood them in good stead. The way of modern Cunas remains rich in custom and belief. Rules of behavior cover nearly every waking activity and are learned from songs and stories that instruct child and adult alike.

Cuna society is matrilineal. A young woman's coming of age is not only important as a ceremonial event but because her marriage to an able young man brings another pair of hands to work for her family. As more men leave the islands for jobs in mainland cities, the women become ever more the conservators of Cuna tradition, especially as expressed through mola making.

Typical Cuna lifestyle is simple and might seem to many Americans to be full of tedious chores. Each morning sees another round of canoeing to the mainland to collect water as there is no fresh water available on the islands. Every day brings more work in the way of picking coconuts or cutting bananas, repairing the thatched roofs of bamboo huts, sweeping out packed earthen floors, washing clothes and sewing on mo-

las. It is the kind of lifestyle that has been described as primitive by those of us whose idea of civilization is rush hour traffic and daily negotiation of the computer screen.

About fifty of the 300 islands of San Blas are inhabited. Because there is not sufficient room on the islands to grow enough food, some planting is done in the coastal forest area. Much of the mainland strip, however, is pristine rain forest. The Cunas believe the land has been entrusted to them in a deeply spiritual sense. Fortunately, the Panamanian government also recognizes their land as Cuna territory. Yet, the forest edges are being nibbled away by surrounding Panamanian farmers.

Outside the Comarca de San Blas, slash-and-burn deforestation techniques are routine. Here, as elsewhere in South America, the desire to produce cheap land quickly often wins out over long-term ecological concerns. Once an area of forest is cut down, the nutrient-poor rain forest soil is useful for planting crops only a few years before it becomes exhausted. Then the farmer must move on and the slash-and-burn process takes place all over again in a new area.

There is some hope, however, for the survival of this rain forest. The Cuna attitude toward the area incorporates religious reverence toward forest spirits as well as faith in medicinal forest-thriving herbs and plants. With international assistance, the region is being developed into a Cuna-run forest park and wildlife preserve. Cuna Indians are being trained as rangers to protect

*Fig. 16-2. Mola with human-type figures and reverse appliqué curlicue patterns. From the David M. Schwartz collection.*

the area and to encourage what one writer calls "scientific tourism."[2]

Spanish explorers arrived at the San Blas Islands early in the 16th century. Their attempts at subjugating the inhabitants led to various atrocities with the result that the Indians withdrew farther into the jungle regions. In time, isolated and largely ignored as they were, legends about them grew.

The eastern coast of Panama was a favorite hideout for pirate ships in the 17th and 18th centuries. The 19th century brought an end to Spanish colonial rule. It also brought regular visits from Yankee whalers and trading ships. Missionaries arrived as well, but their efforts do not seem to have eliminated traditional Cuna worship practices. These focus on an almighty being and afterlife as well as a host of good and bad spirits, medicine men, plant and herb healing, mystical rituals and taboos. According to one Cuna belief, there are many houses in heaven. One is set aside just for artists and mola makers, suggesting the importance with which this needlework is viewed by the people who created it.[3]

## NOTES

1. Ann Wenzel, quoted in article by Johanna McGeary, *Time* (April 14, 1986), p. 31.

2. "Panama: Ever at the Crossroads," *National Geographic* (April 1986), p. 479.

3. Ann Parker and Avon Neal, *Fold Art of the Cuna Indians* (Barre, MA: Barre Publishing Company, 1977), p. 35.

# TECHNIQUES OF THE MOLA

True molas are made only by the San Blas Cuna Indians. There are other branches of the Cuna tribe in Panama, but molas are not part of their tradition.

At first glance, a mola looks as if it were made solely by reverse cut out techniques. That is, it may appear as if the design were entirely built from front to back. In fact,

many molas are a combination of appliqué and reverse appliqué. This means the design is built from middle layer to the back and from the front to the middle layer. Cut outs on cut outs extend both behind a main base fabric and in front of it.

To begin, a base fabric is chosen for the main part of the design. This fabric is cut out in the main design along with the slashes, triangles, and ovals that make up the decorative filling pattern featured on so many molas. Each cut out section of the filling pattern is turned under by hand. Unlike western reverse appliqué, however, a single backing fabric does not show through the filling cut outs. Instead, a different bit of colorful backing is slipped in behind each section of filling. Sections of slashes in red fabric, for instance, are each backed with different colors—one section with blue, one section with green, another with yellow, for example, producing a vibrant effect. In that way the filling decorations are completed.

The main pattern design, also cut out on the base fabric, still remains to be dealt with. It could be backed with a single color. Instead, it is often backed with an additional layer of fabric cut outs which are cut and turned under to show through the first set of cut outs. This gives the main design the effect of having an outline in another color. There may even be more than one outline, depending on how many cut out backing layers are used. Finally, of course, the pattern ends with an uncut backing layer of fabric.

The process, however, is not yet finished. Each large cut out design may be filled in from the front with an appliqué. These appliqués can have layers of smaller appliqués sewn upon them, again repeating the echo effect of many colored outlines in a design. Finally, the topmost layer of exposed fabric may be decorated with embroidery, although this is not always the case. Some molas have little or no embroidery. The finished mola is made up of many, many layers. Some are applied from the back and some from the front.

Colors used are usually rich, deep solids such as azure, magenta, mustard, and emerald, with red, orange, or black predominating (see Plate 16 in the color section). The tropical sun is important in the land of the mola makers and its warmth reaches out to those of us in cooler climates

*Fig. 16-3. Mola with unusual geometric pattern. From the David M. Schwartz collection.*

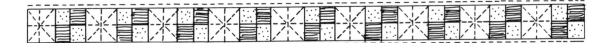

through the rich fiery reds and golden yellows of this needle art. Many molas include words in either English or Spanish, sometimes with the letters appealingly skewed. Innovative spellings may be featured since few mola makers speak any but their own dialect.

Mola making probably got its start a little more than a century ago from the body-painting traditions of Cuna ancestors. It is possible that the influence of early missionaries, with their ideas of what constituted "decent" clothing, coupled with the 19th century availability of bright cloth, needles, and thread led to the establishment of the mola panel. Traders were eager to exchange these simple sewing items for exotic coconuts which found a ready market at home.

The mola blouse of today may have started out as a loose tunic-like dress that hung straight and featured a colorful band around the middle. In time, the band probably became more elaborate, developing into the brightly colored, intricately sewn mola panel, while the tunic dress itself was shortened into a blouse.

Early mola designs were based mostly on floral and abstract motifs harking back to the descriptions that exist of Cuna body painting designs. Over time, the designs became more elaborate. A mola maker's choice of motifs is limited only by her creative instinct today.

As with any handmade article, there are bad molas and good molas. Some western visitors to the area express the concern that, as Cuna-run cooperatives sell more and

*Fig. 16-4. Mola with parrots.*

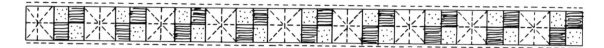

more molas, artistry suffers. Other visitors are pleased that the Cunas have found a way to supplement their income without necessarily resorting to "westernized" ideals and lifestyle. Either way, the mola serves as a bridge between another, very different culture and our own.

# TURTLE POCKET PURSE         Difficulty Level: Moderate

Please see Appliqué and Binding in the chapter on Basic Techniques before beginning.

A pocket purse is useful when you want to carry a few small items with you but do not want the encumbrance of a regular purse. Traditionally, mola panels form the front and back of a Cuna woman's blouse. But molas are quickly moving out of their traditional sphere. Many visitors to Panama regard the mola as such a unique and exquisite art form that they frame the panels for display. Cuna women, finding a ready market for small items made in mola-style

*Fig. 16-5. Mola Pocket Purse project (see cover for color).*

## TEMPLATE DIAGRAM

*Templates for this project look like this and are found at the back of the book.*

layered reverse appliqué, have responded by making and selling a variety of small hand sewn projects.

This little project does not pretend to be a real mola, but will give you a feel for working in layered reverse appliqué. The most time-consuming aspect of its technique is the slashings in which a layer of contrasting color is slipped beneath a turned-under slash in the fabric. Depending on how much time you want to spend, you can follow the suggestion for placement of the slashings, or use fewer slashings and position them in your own pattern on the purse front.

## MATERIALS

14" × 10" magenta fabric rectangle (purse lining)
Two 7" × 10" magenta fabric rectangles (purse front and purse back)
7" × 10" aqua rectangle
1" × 16" aqua fabric strip (purse opening)
1" × 36" strip magenta fabric (purse strap)
Assorted solid fabric scraps: red, purple, lavender, cobalt blue
Thread to match fabrics—especially the magenta

## DIRECTIONS

1. Place the magenta purse front on top of the aqua rectangle. Each rectangle should be right side up. Using the templates provided for this project, draw the outlines for the turtle, butterfly, and fish onto the magenta fabric. Use the diagram as a guide in positioning your animal shapes freehand. Pin the two fabrics together, then baste around the outside of the turtle and butterfly. (We will get to the fish in a moment.) Your basting stitches should be about a ½" outside each marked design.

2. Holding the basted fabric layers so that the magenta is on top and the aqua is on the bottom, use a pair of sharp, pointed scissors

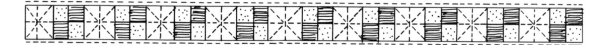

to trim away the magenta fabric ¼″ inside the marked design. Be sure not to cut through to the aqua fabric layer. Iris scissors work well for this and are available at pharmacies that sell surgical supplies. Clip the curves and corners of the turtle and butterfly designs right to the marked line.

3. Using magenta thread, turn under the ¼″ margin of each design and sew to the aqua layer. Use the point of the needle to "roll" or turn under the raw fabric edges. Bring the thread up through the fold that is created by the turned under edge, then run the needle back down through the aqua layer beneath. This will create an almost invisible appliqué stitch. Sew all the way around the turtle and butterfly so that the magenta layer is completely sewn to the aqua layer and there are no raw fabric edges showing. Remove the basting stitches.

4. Turn your project over so that the aqua side is facing up. Trim away the excess aqua fabric around each design. Leave a ¼″ to ½″ margin of aqua around both the sewn turtle and butterfly outlines.

5. Follow the above process for the fish outline which is already marked on your magenta purse front. This time, however, use red fabric to back the design. Baste the magenta to the red, trim fabric from inside the design, clipping curves to the marked line. Use a "rolling needle" technique to turn under the raw magenta fabric edges and sew to the red fabric. Remove the bast-

ing stitches. Turn over the project and trim away the excess red fabric around the outside of the sewn design outline.

6. Place the project face down on a terry-cloth towel and iron from the back.

7. To finish the turtle's back you will use the three turtleback circle templates and the small cross. Center and mark the largest circle on the turtle's back. Cut a small square of red fabric about 4″ × 4″. Pin and baste this under the marked circle. Be sure there is a ¼″ to ½″ margin of red all around the outside of the circle. Now cut the aqua fabric layer all around the inside of the circle, leaving a ¼″ margin. Be sure not to cut the red fabric underneath. Clip the circle to the marked line for ease in turning under.

8. Using matching thread and a "rolling needle" technique, turn under the raw edge of the aqua fabric circle and sew to the red fabric underneath. Turn the project over then trim away the excess red fabric, leaving a ½″ margin around the outside of the sewn fish outline.

9. At this point, please take note that one could accomplish this much of the project using *multiple* layers instead of just two layers at a time. Having mastered the simplified technique in this beginner's project, you can feel confident about producing similar effects more efficiently with multiple fabric layers should you go on to design your own mola. Up to this point, your design has

been "built up" from the back by reverse appliqué. Now the cut outs are to be further embellished from the front with conventional appliqué shapes. Use the smaller turtleback templates, two small circles and the cross, to mark and cut out your fabric appliqués. To follow the project sample exactly, use blue for the larger of the two circles, purple for the smaller one, and aqua for the cross. Turn under the outside edge of each shape, pin, and sew in place using matching thread.

10. Follow the above process for the inner shapes for the butterfly and fish. Mark, cut out, position, and sew in place. Turn the project over and iron on a towel before continuing on to the slashings.

11. Most pictorial molas are characterized by an all-over pattern of tiny colorful cut out shapes. These may be triangles, straight slashes, or squares. Bright colors show through the cut outs which are themselves so small that they create a sparkle effect. This project calls for straight slashings, but if you go on to produce a mola of your own, you will want to experiment with other tiny cut outs. To begin the slashings, follow the diagram and mark the slashings freehand on the magenta top. You do not need to measure, but leave plenty of outer margin. Be sure not to place a slashing less than 1″ away from the outer fabric edge.

12. Work in groups of three slashings at a time. Baste a small piece of contrasting fabric behind a group of slashing cut marks. Then cut the slashings, taking care not to cut through to the second layer. Use matching thread and a rolling needle technique to turn under the raw edge of each slashing just as you did when working with the larger animal shapes. As you finish one group of three slashings go on to the next, using a different bright solid color to show through each group of three.

13. When all of the slashings are done, the mola portion of the project is complete. It is now ready to be made into a pocket purse. With right sides together, sew the mola purse top to the purse back along the two long insides and the bottom. Turn right side out. Fold the magenta lining fabric in half so that it forms a 7″ × 10″ rectangle with right sides inside. Sew down one long side and one short side. You now have a liner pocket and an outer mola pocket. Keeping right sides inside, position the lining pocket inside the outer pocket and pin. Trim the raw edges at the top (the opening of the purse) so that they are even. Bind the opening with the strip of aqua fabric.

14. Fold and pin the strip of magenta fabric for the purse strap. It should be folded in half and then the raw edges folded inside and against each other. Sew the fold of the purse strap closed. Position one end of the strap at the top left of the pocket purse and the other at the top right. Fold under the raw ends of the strap and sew in place to complete the project.

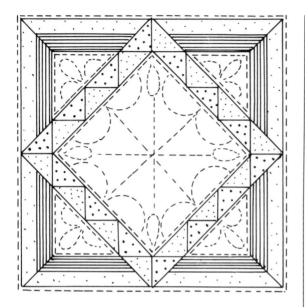

# Recommended Reading

There are so many fine books on quilting and related sewing techniques—particularly general instruction books—that it is impossible to include here even a representative number. Instead, the following books are recommended for readers who, intrigued by the sampling of an indigenous needlework technique, may wish to learn more about it. A few books have also been included that focus primarily on the culture in which a specific style developed, rather than on the needlework itself, or are simply "idea books" that lend themselves to a particular technique. These have been marked by an asterisk.

## Piecing and Appliquéing

*American Pieced Quilts*, Jonathan Holstein, New York: Viking Press, 1972.

*Hearts and Hands: The Influence of Women and Quilts on American Society*, Pat Ferrero, Elaine Hedges, Julie Silber, San Francisco: Quilt Digest Press, 1987.*

*The Kids' Very Own Quilt Book*, Willow Ann Soltow, Lombard, IL: Wallace-Homestead, 1986.

*Quilts in America*, Patsy and Myron Orlofsky, New York: McGraw Hill, 1974.

*Remember Me—Women and Their Friendship Quilts*, Linda Otto Lipsett, San Francisco: The Quilt Digest Press, 1985.*

*The Standard Book of Quiltmaking and Colleting*, Marguerite Ickis, New York: Dover, 1959.

# Crazy Quilts

*American Patchwork Quilts*, Lenice Ingram Bacon, NY: Bonanza Books, 1980.

*Crazy Quilt Stitches*, Dorothy Bond, published by D. Bond, 34706 Row River Road, Cottage Grove, OR, 97424.

*Crazy Quilts*, Penny McMorris, New York: E.P. Dutton, 1984.

# Amish Quilts

*An Amish Adventure: A Workbook for Color in Quilts*, Roberta Horton, Lafayette, CA: C & T Publishing, 1983.

*Amish Crib Quilts*, Rachel and Kenneth Pellman, Intercourse, PA: Good Books, 1985.

*The Amish Quilt*, Eve Wheatcroft Grannick, Intercourse, PA: Good Books, 1989.

*A Gallery of Amish Quilts*, Robert Bishop and Elizabeth Safanda, New York: E.P. Dutton, 1976.

*The World of Amish Quilts*, Rachel and Kenneth Pellman, Intercourse, PA: Good Books, 1984.

# Seminole Piecing

*Big Cypress: A Changing Seminole Community*, New York: Holt, Rinehart, and Winston, 1972.*

*The Complete Book of Patchwork, Quilting, and Appliqué*, Linda Seward, New York: Prentice Hall, 1987.

*Seminole Patchwork*, Margaret Brandebourg, New York: Sterling Publishing, 1987.

*The Seminole Patchwork Book*, Cheryl Greider Bradkin, Atlanta GA: Yours Truly, 1980.

# Hawaiian Quilting

*Hawaiian Quilting, A Fine Art*, Elizabeth Akana, Honolulu: Exhibition catalog of the Mission House Museum, 1981.

*Hawaiian Quilting on Kauai*, Edith Rice Plews, Kauai: Kauai Museum Publications, 1973.

*The Quilt Digest, Volume 2*, San Francisco: Kirakofe and Kile, 1984.

*Quilting II*, Penny McMorris, Bowling Green, OH: Bowling Green State University, guide to accompany the television series produced by WBGU-TV, 1982.

*Your Hawaiian Quilt: How to Make It*, Helen Inns, Honolulu: Hawaii Home Demonstration Council, 1957.

# Tifaifai

*The Cut-outs of Henri Matisse*, John Elderfield, New York: George Braziller, 1978.*

*Patterns from Paradise*, Vicki Poggioli, Pittstown, NJ: Mainstreet Press, 1988.

*Tifaifai and the Quilts of Polynesia*, Joyce D. Hammond, Honolulu: University of Hawaii Press, 1986.

# Hmong Patchwork

*Creating Pa Ndau Appliqué*, Carla Hassel, Lombard, IL: Wallace-Homestead Book Company, 1984.

*Hearts of Sorrow: Vietnamese-American Lives*,

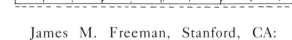

James M. Freeman, Stanford, CA: Stanford University Press, 1989.*

# Sashiko

*Japanese Quilts*, Jill Liddell and Yuko Watanabe, New York: E.P. Dutton, 1989.*

*Sashiko*, Bonnie Benjamin, Glendale, CA: Needlearts International, 1986.

*Sashiko Quilting*, Kimi Ota, Seattle, WA: 1981.

# Shisha Appliqué

*The Art of Appliqué*, Marie-Janine Solvit, New York: Arco Publishing, 1984.

*Dowries from Kutch: A Woman's Folk Art Tradition in India*, Vickie C. Elson, Los Angeles, CA: Museum of Cultural History, UCLA, 1975.*

# West African Appliqué

*African Textiles and Decorative Arts*, New York: Museum of Modern Art, 1972.*

*Making Animal Quilts*, Willow Ann Soltow, Intercourse, PA: Good Books, 1986.*

*Quilting II*, Penny McMorris, Bowling Green, OH: Bowling Green State University, guide to accompany the television series produced by WBGU-TV, 1982.

*Who'd A Thought It*, Eli Leon, Catalog to the exhibition at the San Francisco Craft and Folk Art Museum, 1989.*

# Trapunto

*Trapunto and Other Forms of Raised Quilting*, Mary Morgan and Dee Mosteller, New York: Charles Scribner's Sons, 1977.

*Quilting*, Averil Colby, New York: Charles Scribner's Sons, 1971.

*Quilting, Patchwork, Appliqué, and Trapunto*, Thelma R. Newman, New York: Crown Publishers, 1974.

# English Piecing

*Copycats*, Marianne Ford, London: Andrew Deutsch, 1983.

*Geometric Patterns from Roman Mosaics*, Robert Field, Norfolk, England: Tarquin Publications, 1988.*

*Patchwork*, Averil Colby, London, B.T. Batsford, 1958.

*Patchwork from Mosaics*, Helen Fairfield, London, B.T. Batsford, 1985.*

*The Quilts of the British Isles*, Janet Rae, New York: E.P. Dutton, 1987.*

*Traditional British Quilts*, Dorothy Osler, London: B.T. Batsford, 1987.*

# Broderie Perse

*The Complete Book of Patchwork, Quilting, and Appliqué*, Linda Seward, New York: Prentice Hall, 1987.

*Nineteenth-Century Appliqué Quilts*, Dilys Blum and Jack L. Lindsey, from *The Bulletin*, Philadelphia Museum of Art, vol. 85, Fall 1989.

*The Pieced Quilt: An American Tradition*, Jonathan Holstein, Boston: Little, Brown, and Company, 1973.

# Arpilleras

*Scraps of Life: Chilean Arpilleras*, Marjorie Agosin, translated by Cola Franzen, Trenton, NJ: Red Sea Press, 1987.

# Molas

*The Complete Book of Patchwork, Quilting, and Appliqué*, Linda Seward, New York: Prentice Hall, 1987.

*The Great Noank Quilt Factory: How to Make Quilts and Quilted Things*, Sharon McKain, New York: Random House, 1974. (see reverse appliqué)

*Molas: Folk Art of the Cuna Indians*, Ann Parker and Avon Neal, New York: Crown: 1977.*

# Supplies and Suppliers

(**Note:** The following listings were adapted with permission from *The Complete Book of Machine Embroidery* by Robbie and Tony Fanning [Chilton, 1986].)

# Threads

**Note:** Ask your local retailer or send a pre-addressed stamped envelope to the companies below to find out where to buy their threads.

### EXTRA-FINE

Assorted threads
　　Robison-Anton Textile Co.
　　175 Bergen Blvd.
　　Fairview, NJ 07022

DMC 100% cotton, Sizes 30 and 50
　　The DMC Corporation
　　107 Trumbull Street
　　Elizabeth, NJ 07206

Dual-Duty Plus Extra-fine, cotton-wrapped polyester
　　J&P Coats/Coats & Clark
　　30 Patewood Dr., Suite 351
　　Greenville, SC 29615

Madeira threads
　　Madeira Co.
　　56 Primrose Drive
　　O'Shea Industrial Park
　　Laconia, NH 03246

Mettler Metrosene Fine Machine Embroidery cotton, Size 60/2
　　Swiss-Metrosene, Inc.
　　Wm. E. Wright Co.
　　South Street
　　West Warren, MA 01092

Natesh 100% rayon, lightweight
Aardvark Adventures
PO Box 2449
Livermore, CA 94550

Paradise 100% rayon
D&E Distributing
199 N. El Camino Real #F-242
Encinitas, CA 92024

Sulky 100% rayon, Sizes 30 and 40
Speed Stitch, Inc.
PO Box 3472
Port Charlotte, FL 33949

Zwicky 100% cotton, Size 30/2
White Sewing Machine Co.
11750 Berea Rd.
Cleveland, OH 44111

## ORDINARY

Dual Duty Plus, cotton-wrapped
polyester—*see* Dual Duty Plus Extra-fine

Also Natesh heavyweight, Zwicky in
cotton and polyester, Mettler Metrosene
in 30/2, 40/3, 50/3, and 30/3, and
Metrosene Plus

## METALLIC

Madeira Co. (see address above)

Troy Thread & Textile Corp.
2300 W. Diversey Ave.
Chicago, IL 60647
Free catalog

YLI Corporation
45 West 300 North
Provo, UT 84601

# Quilting Supplies

Aardvark Adventures
PO Box 2449
Livermore, CA 94550
Also publishes "Aardvark
Territorial Enterprise"

The Cloth Cupboard
Box 2263
Boise, ID 83701
(A wide variety of specialized
quilting supplies including
Japanese silk pins useful for
crazy patchwork and other
intricate needlework, and
"Chalkoner" chalk wheels for
marking fabric.)

Clotilde Inc.
1909 SW First Ave.
Ft. Lauderdale, FL 33315

Craft Gallery Ltd.
PO Box 8319
Salem, MA 01971

D&E Distributing
199 N. El Camino Read #F-242
Encinitas, CA 92024

Verna Holt's Machine Stitchery
PO Box 236
Hurricane, UT 84734

Lacis
2982 Adeline St.
Berkeley, CA 94703

Nancy's Notions
PO Box 683
Beaver Dam, WI 53916
    Catalog $.60 in stamps

Patty Lou Creations
Rt. 2, Box 90-A
Elgin, OR 97827

Sew-Art International
PO Box 550
Bountiful, UT 84010
    Catalog $2

Speed Stitch, Inc.
PO Box 3472
Port Charlotte, FL 33952
    Catalog $2

SewCraft
Box 1869
Warsaw, IN 46580
    Also publishers newsletter/
    catalog

Treadleart
25834 Narbonne Ave.
Lomita, CA 90717

# Miscellaneous

Applications
871 Fourth Ave.
Sacramento, CA 95818
    Release Paper for appliqué

Clearbrook Woolen Shop
PO Box 8
Clearbrook, VA 22624
    Ultrasuede scraps

The Fabric Carr
170 State St.
Los Altos, CA 94022
    Sewing gadgets

The Green Pepper Inc.
941 Olive Street
Eugene, OR 97401
    Outdoor fabrics, patterns—
    $1 catalog

Home-Sew
Bethlehem, PA 18018
    Lace—$.25 catalog

Kasuri Dyeworks
1915 Shattuck Avenue
Berkeley, CA 94704
    Examples of sashiko, sashiko
    supplies and Japanese fabrics

Libby's Creations
PO Box 16800 Ste. 180
Mesa, AZ 85202
    Horizontal spool holder

LJ Originals, Inc.
516 Sumac Pl.
DeSoto, TX 75115
    TransGraph

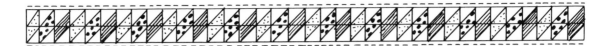

Needlearts International
P.O. Box 6447
Dept. CP1
Glendale, CA 91225
    Catalog $2 (yearly subscription)
    Sashiko yarn and templates

Newark Dressmaker Supply
PO Box 2248
Lehigh Valley, PA 18001

Osage Country Quilt Factory
400 Walnut
Overbrook, KS 66524
    Washable fabric spray glue

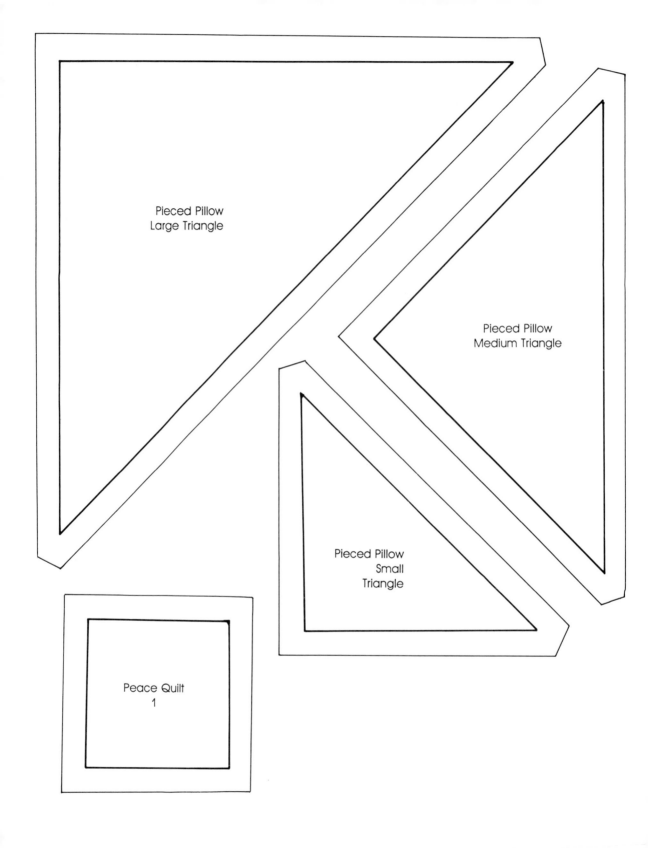

Pieced Pillow
Large Triangle

Pieced Pillow
Medium Triangle

Pieced Pillow
Small
Triangle

Peace Quilt
1

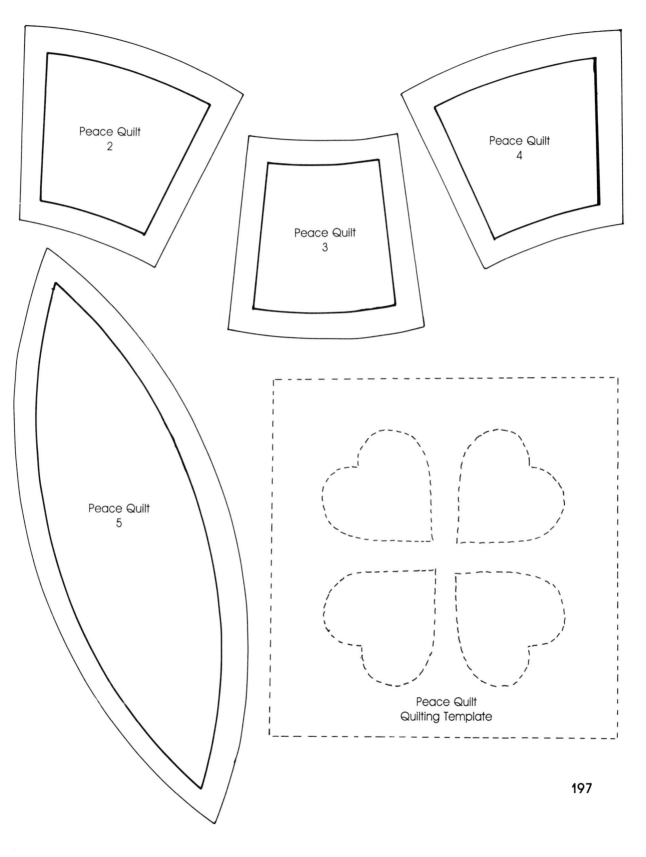

Peace Quilt
2

Peace Quilt
3

Peace Quilt
4

Peace Quilt
5

Peace Quilt
Quilting Template

197

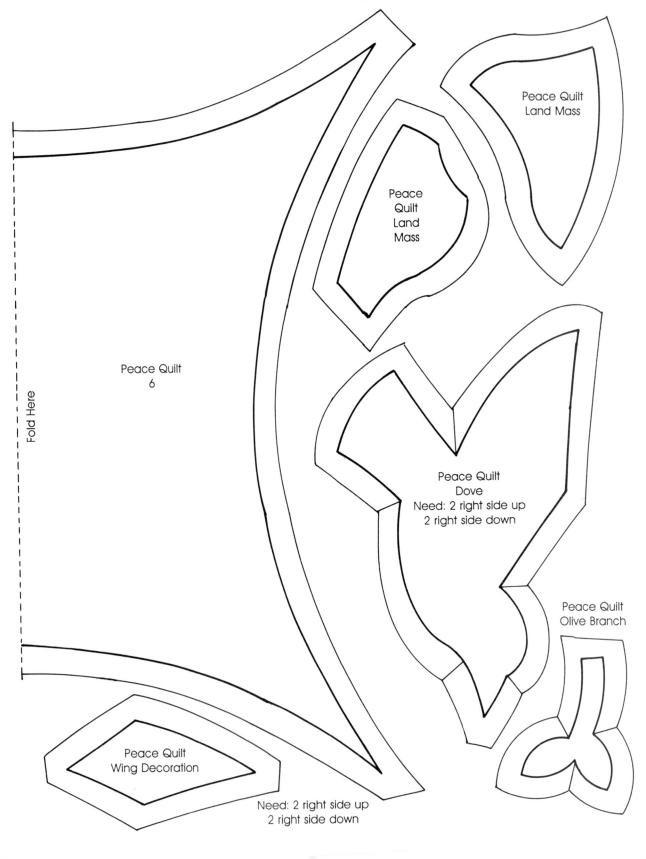

Peace Quilt
Land Mass

Peace
Quilt
Land
Mass

Fold Here

Peace Quilt
6

Peace Quilt
Dove
Need: 2 right side up
2 right side down

Peace Quilt
Olive Branch

Peace Quilt
Wing Decoration

Need: 2 right side up
2 right side down

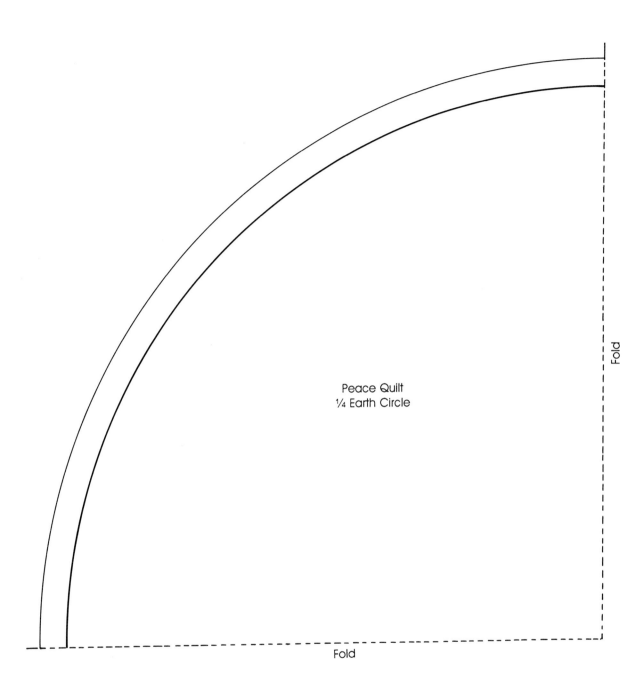

Peace Quilt
¼ Earth Circle

Fold

Fold

199

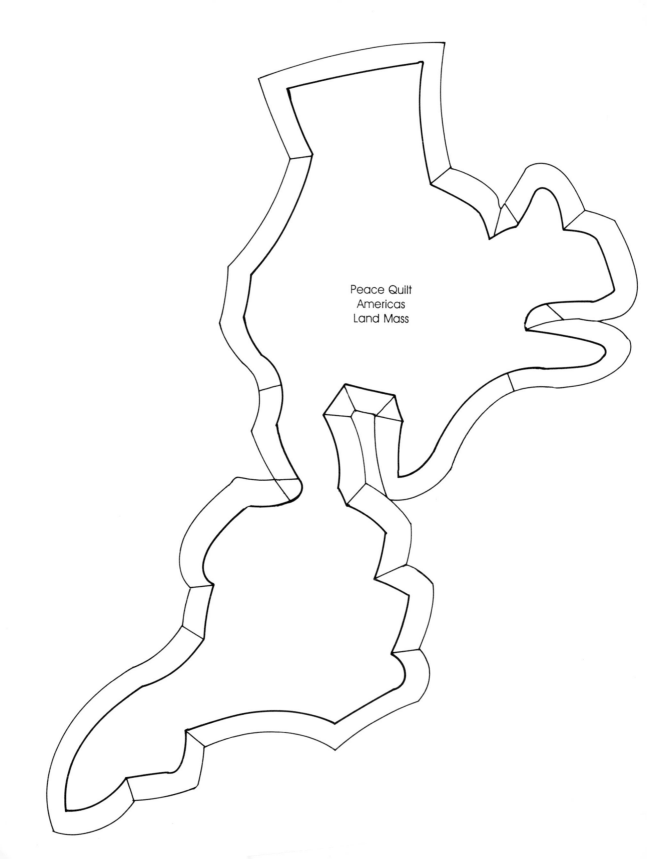

Peace Quilt
Americas
Land Mass

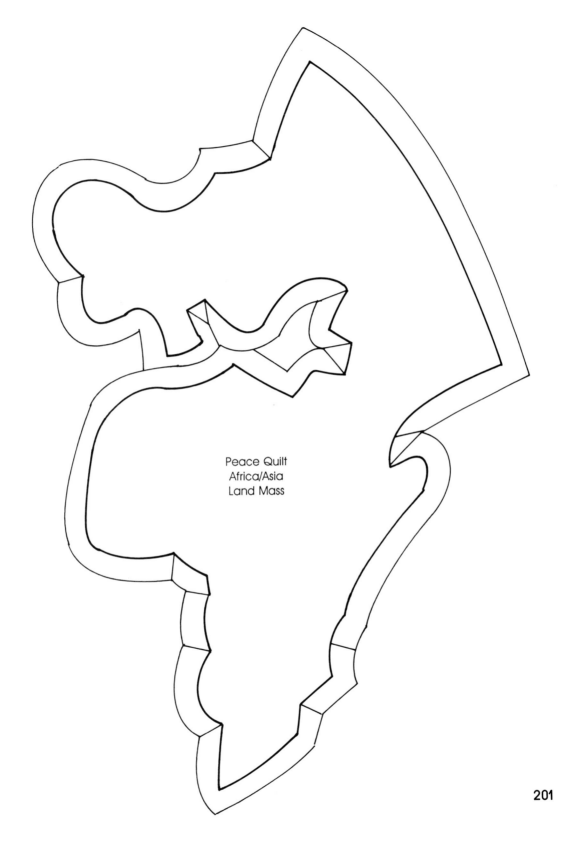

Peace Quilt
Africa/Asia
Land Mass

201

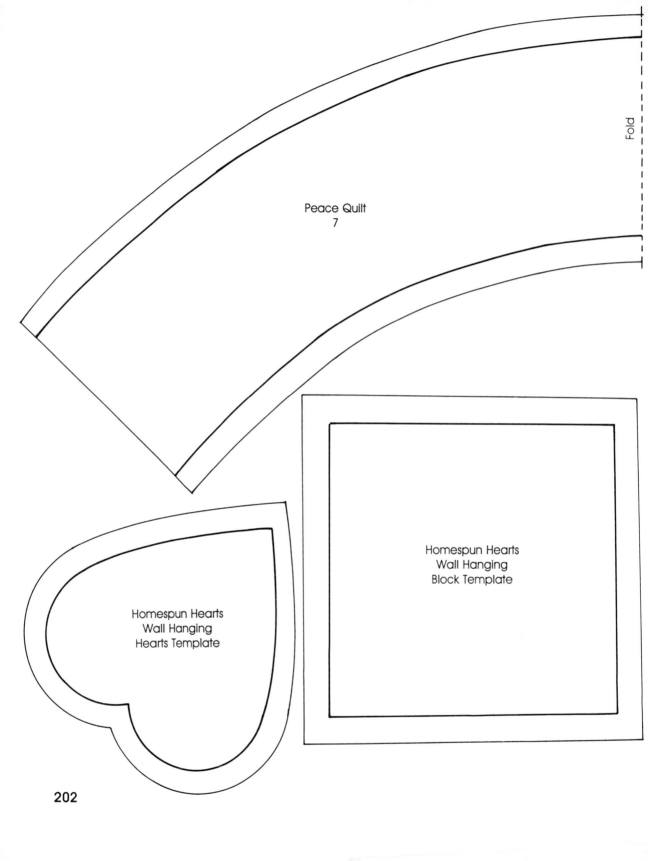

Peace Quilt
7

Fold

Homespun Hearts
Wall Hanging
Hearts Template

Homespun Hearts
Wall Hanging
Block Template

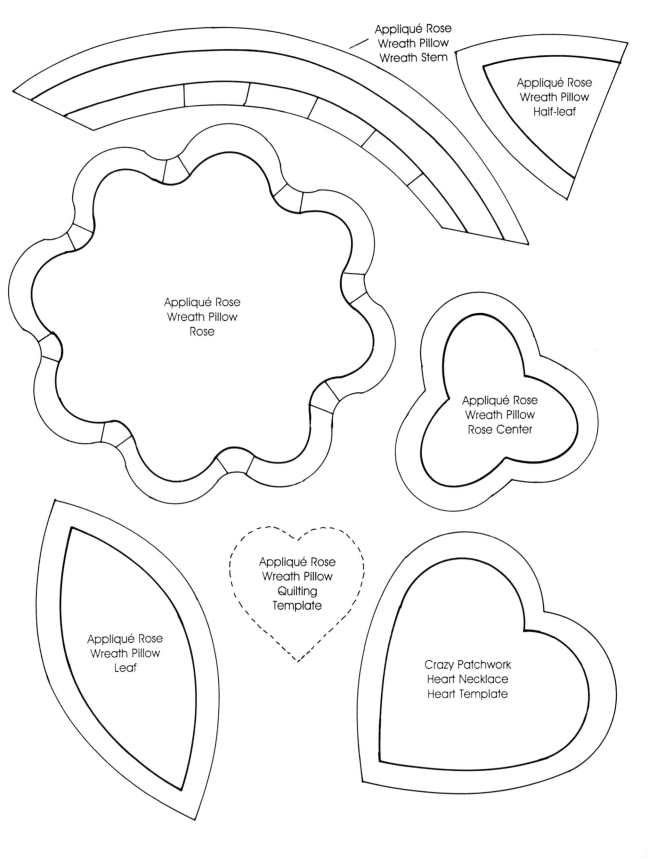

Appliqué Rose
Wreath Pillow
Wreath Stem

Appliqué Rose
Wreath Pillow
Half-leaf

Appliqué Rose
Wreath Pillow
Rose

Appliqué Rose
Wreath Pillow
Rose Center

Appliqué Rose
Wreath Pillow
Leaf

Appliqué Rose
Wreath Pillow
Quilting
Template

Crazy Patchwork
Heart Necklace
Heart Template

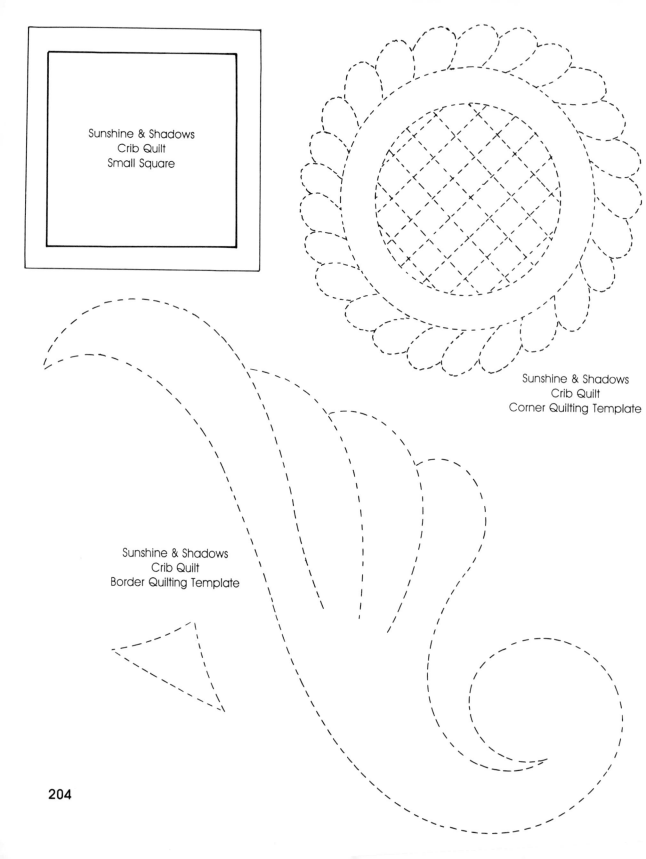

Sunshine & Shadows
Crib Quilt
Small Square

Sunshine & Shadows
Crib Quilt
Corner Quilting Template

Sunshine & Shadows
Crib Quilt
Border Quilting Template

204

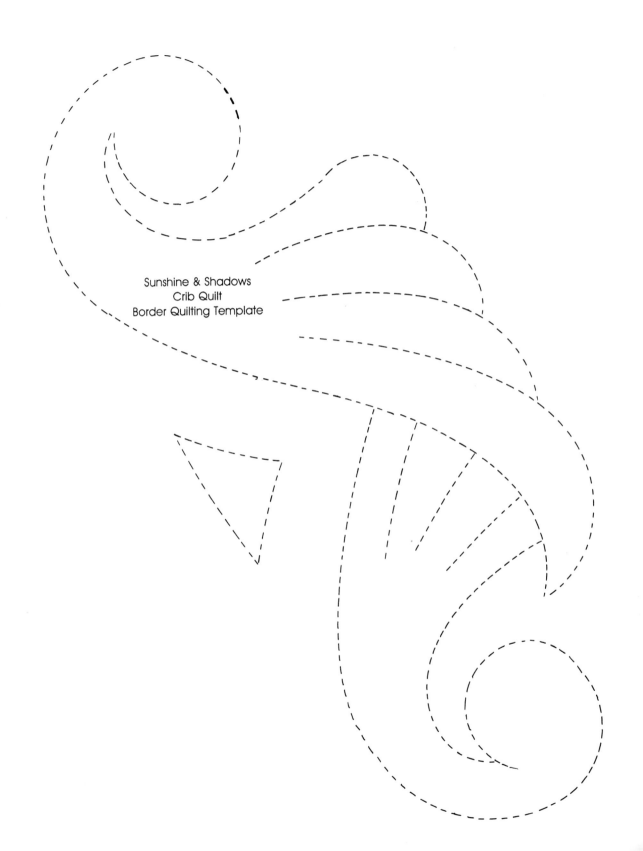

Sunshine & Shadows
Crib Quilt
Border Quilting Template

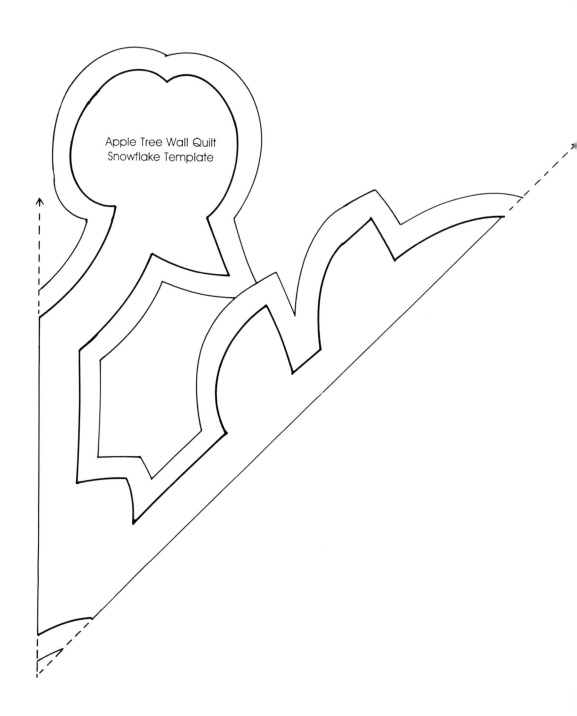

Apple Tree Wall Quilt
Snowflake Template

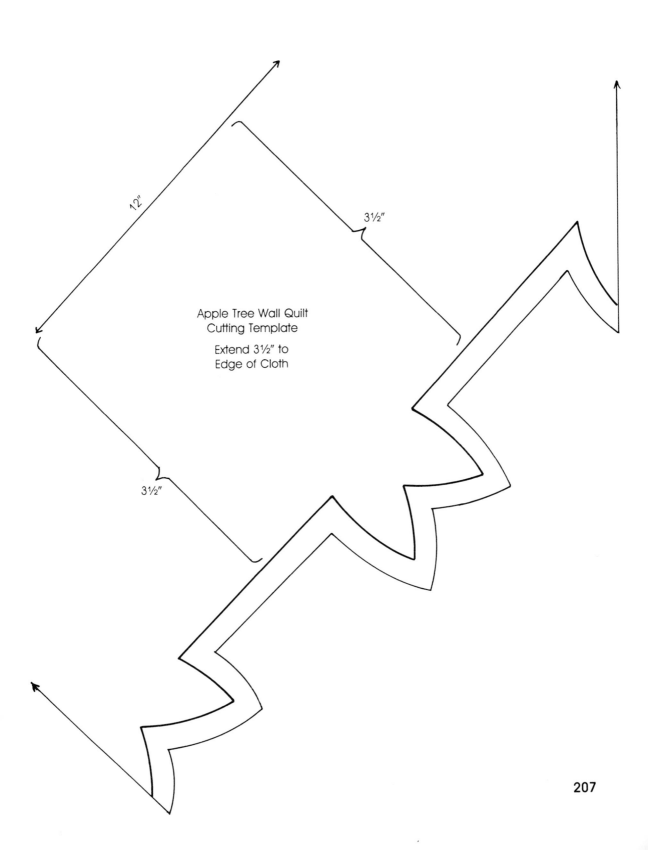

12"

3½"

Apple Tree Wall Quilt
Cutting Template

Extend 3½" to
Edge of Cloth

3½"

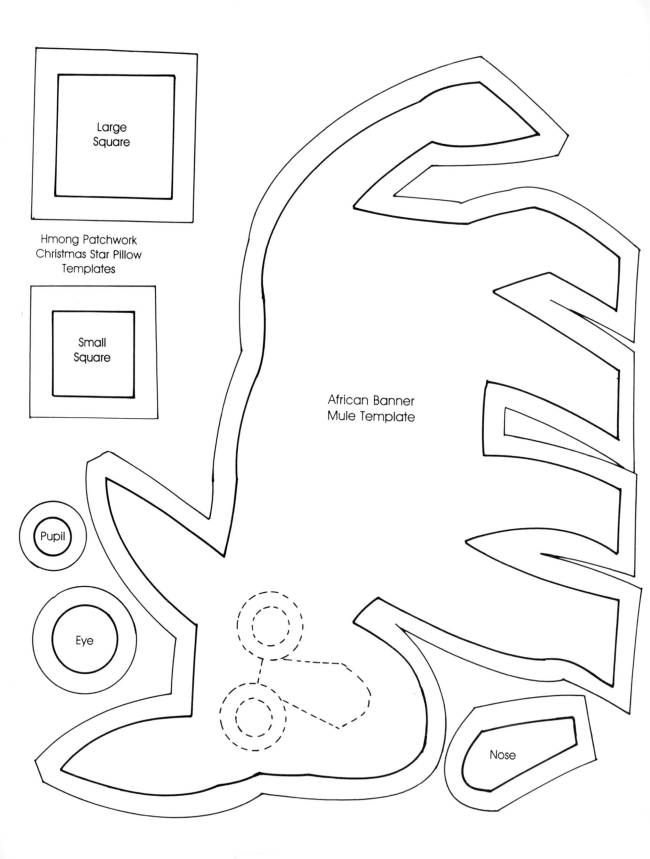

Large
Square

Hmong Patchwork
Christmas Star Pillow
Templates

Small
Square

African Banner
Mule Template

Pupil

Eye

Nose

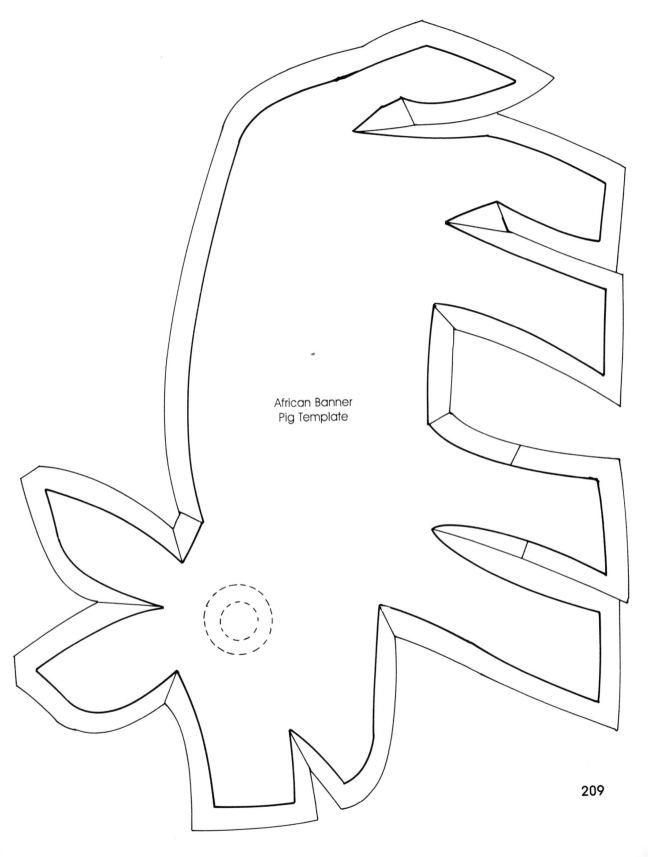

African Banner
Pig Template

209

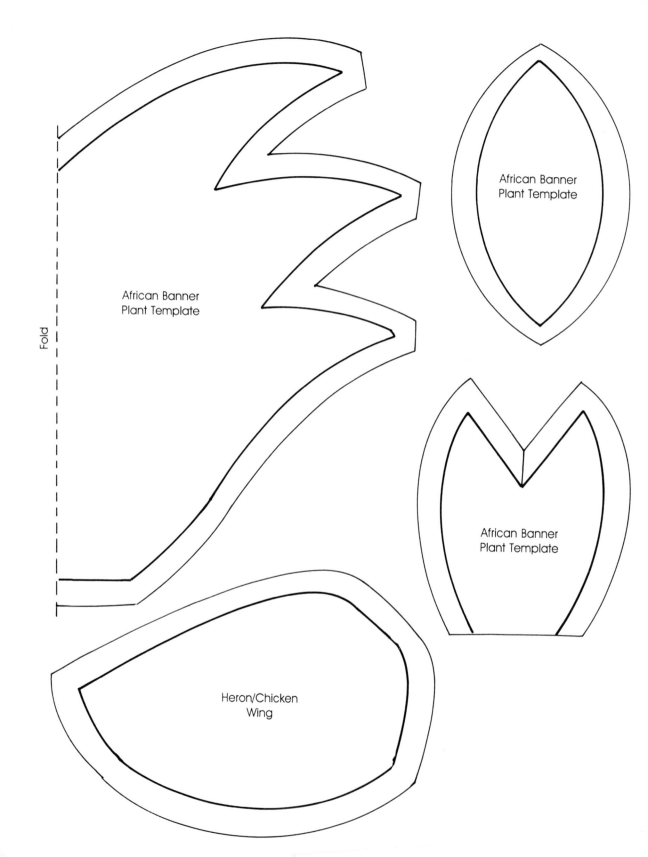

Fold

African Banner
Plant Template

African Banner
Plant Template

African Banner
Plant Template

Heron/Chicken
Wing

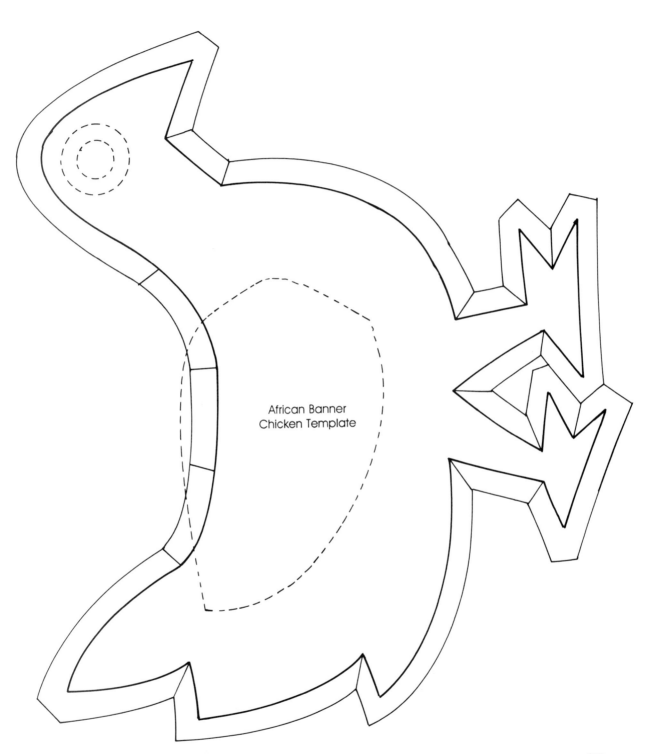

African Banner
Chicken Template

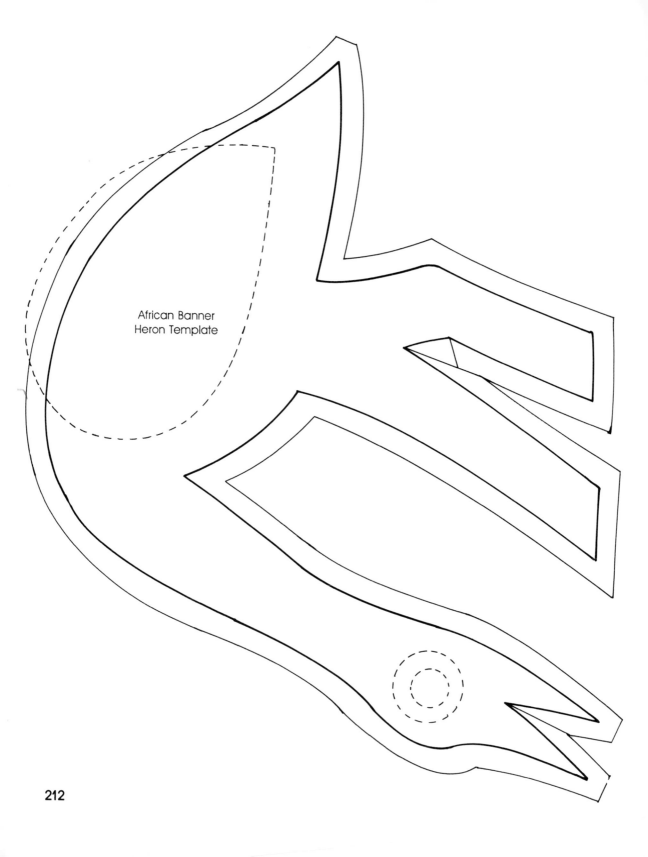

African Banner
Heron Template

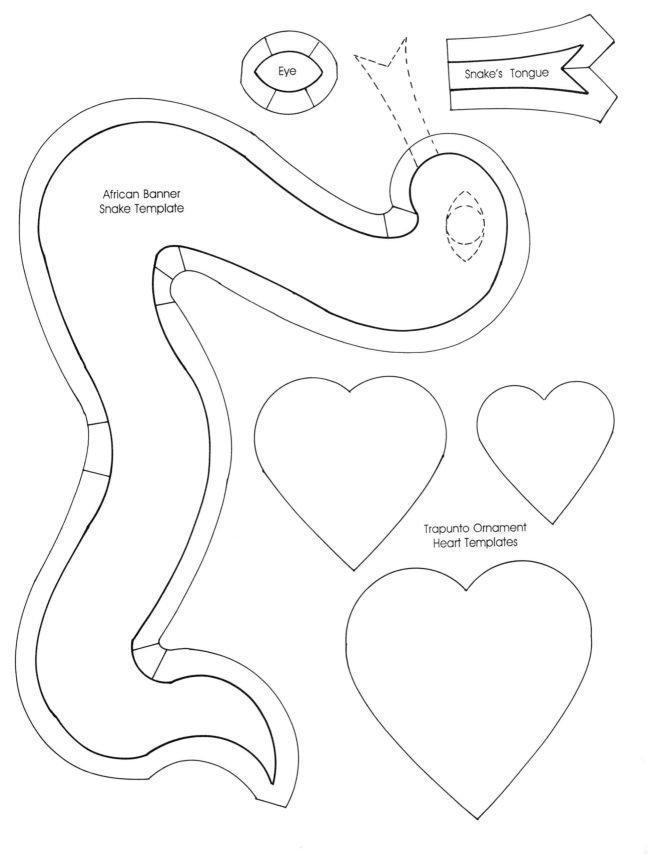

Eye

Snake's Tongue

African Banner
Snake Template

Trapunto Ornament
Heart Templates

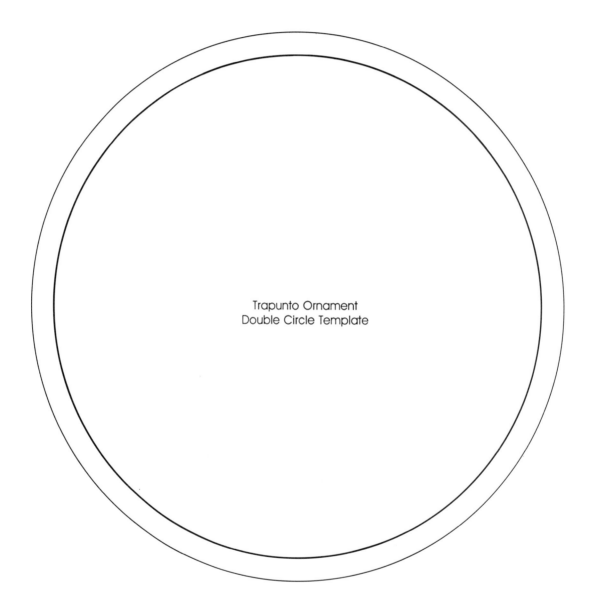

Trapunto Ornament
Double Circle Template

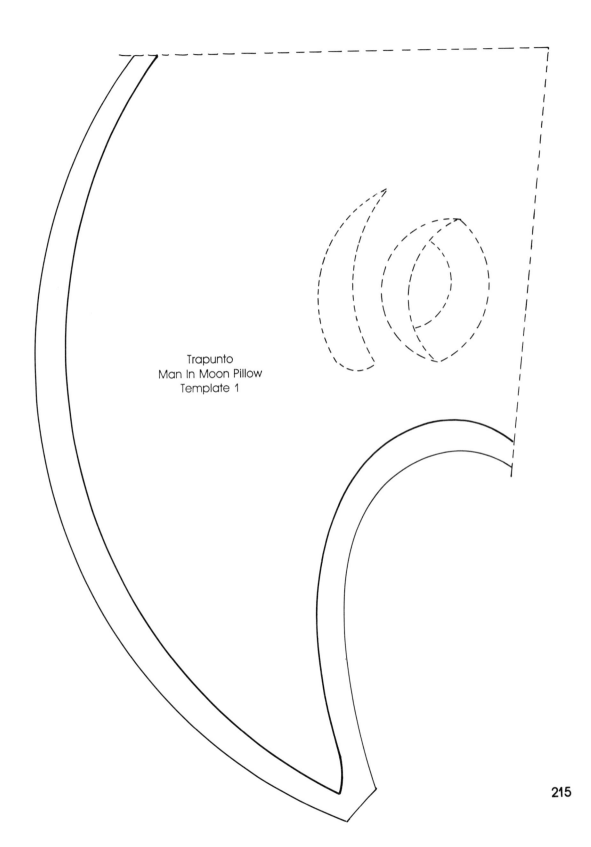

Trapunto
Man In Moon Pillow
Template 1

215

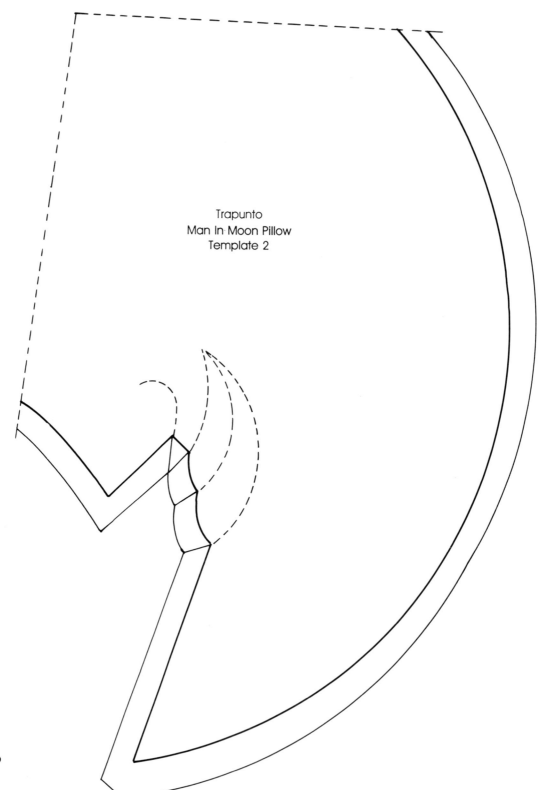

Trapunto
Man In Moon Pillow
Template 2

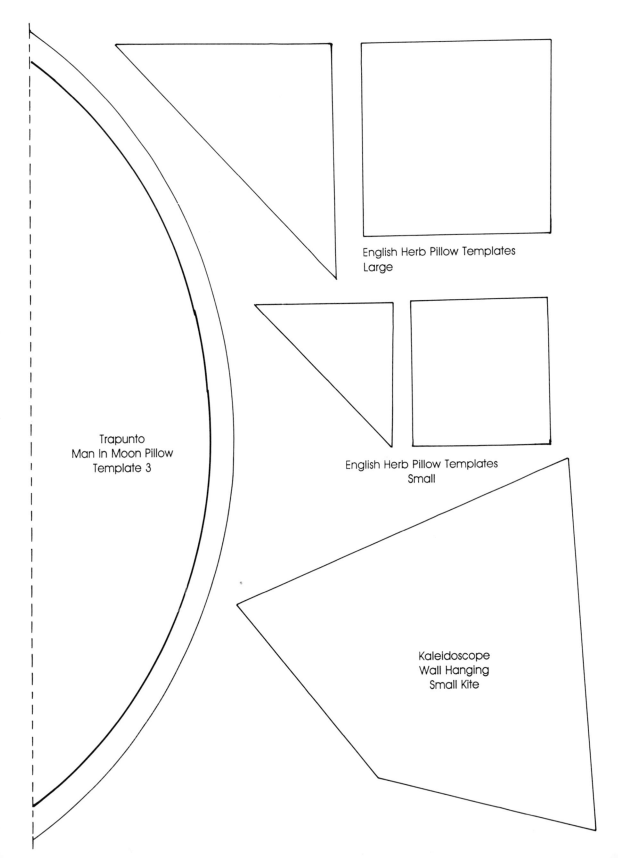

English Herb Pillow Templates
Large

Trapunto
Man In Moon Pillow
Template 3

English Herb Pillow Templates
Small

Kaleidoscope
Wall Hanging
Small Kite

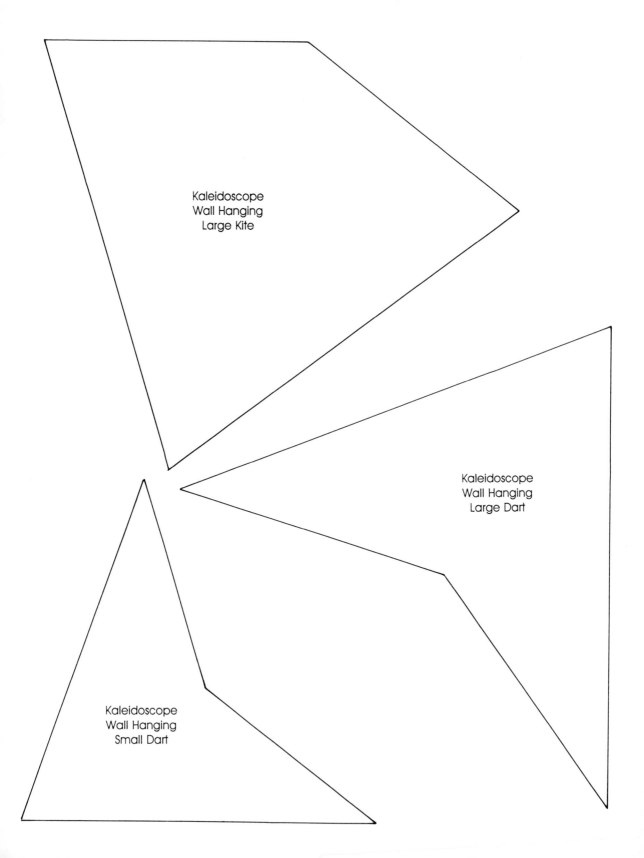

Kaleidoscope
Wall Hanging
Large Kite

Kaleidoscope
Wall Hanging
Large Dart

Kaleidoscope
Wall Hanging
Small Dart

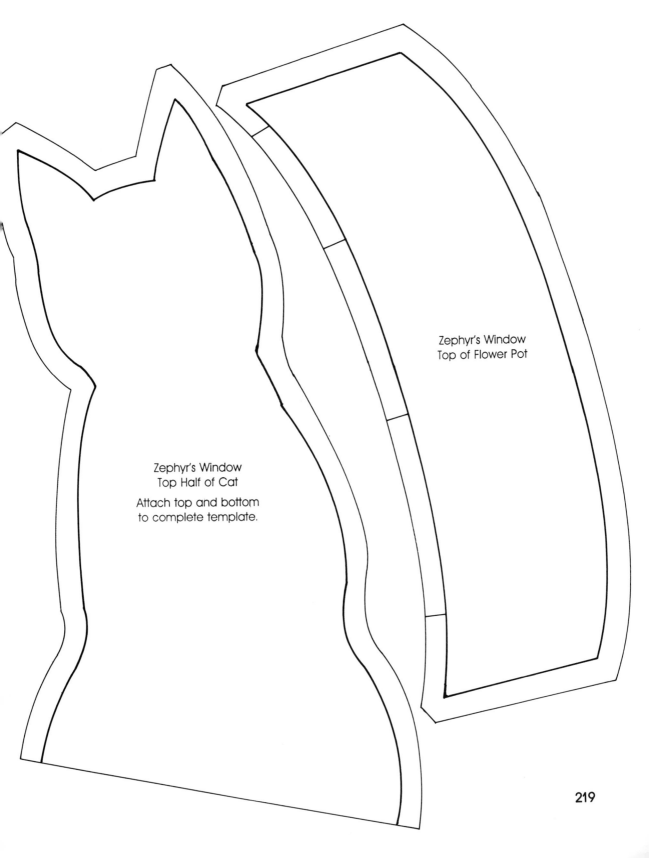

Zephyr's Window
Top Half of Cat

Attach top and bottom
to complete template.

Zephyr's Window
Top of Flower Pot

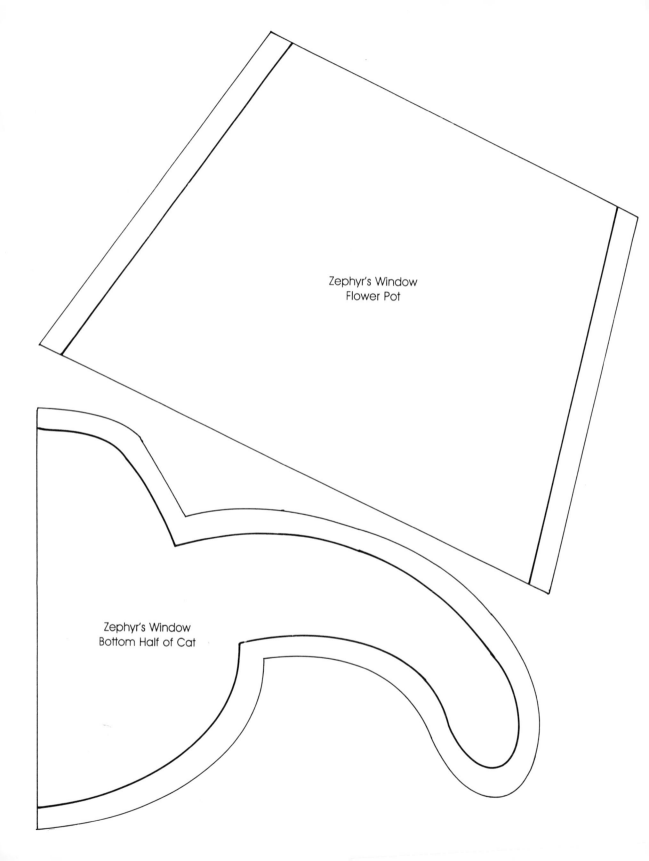

Zephyr's Window
Flower Pot

Zephyr's Window
Bottom Half of Cat

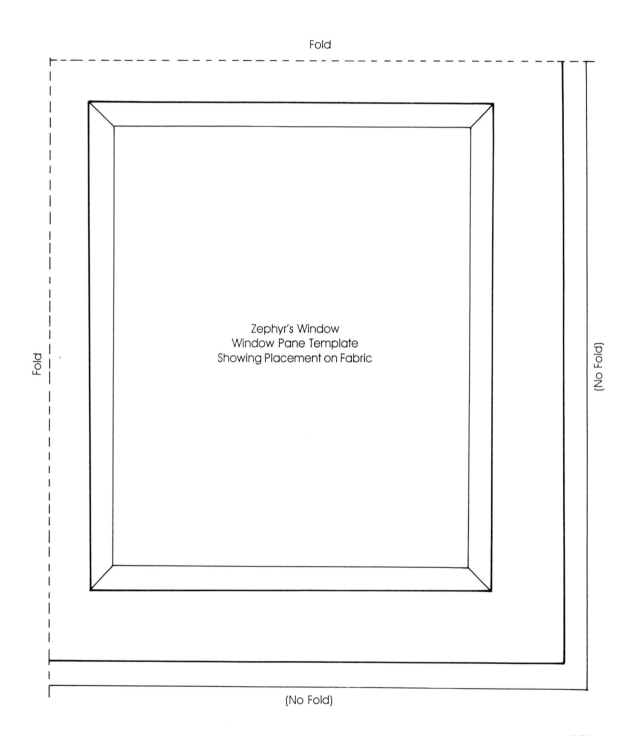

Fold

Fold

(No Fold)

Zephyr's Window
Window Pane Template
Showing Placement on Fabric

(No Fold)

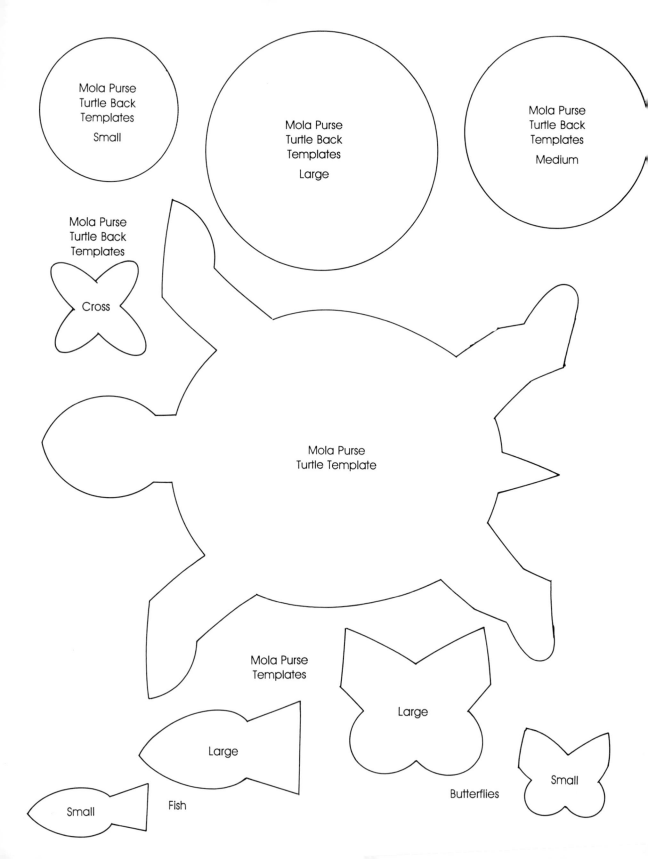

Mola Purse
Turtle Back
Templates

Small

Mola Purse
Turtle Back
Templates

Large

Mola Purse
Turtle Back
Templates

Medium

Mola Purse
Turtle Back
Templates

Cross

Mola Purse
Turtle Template

Mola Purse
Templates

Large

Large

Small

Fish

Butterflies

Small

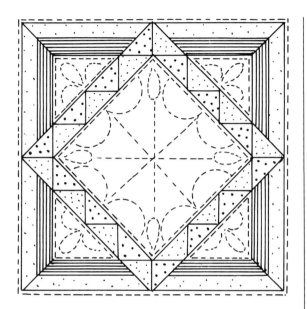

# Index

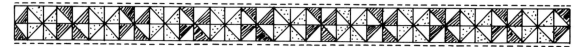

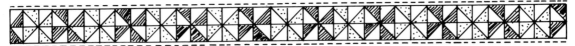